TEXT AND INTERPRETATION

NUMBERS

A PRACTICAL COMMENTARY

B. MAARSINGH

Translated by John Vriend

GRAND RAPIDS, MICHIGAN
WILLIAM B. EERDMANS PUBLISHING COMPANY

Copyright © 1987 by Wm. B. Eerdmans Publishing Co.
255 Jefferson Ave. S.E., Grand Rapids, Mich. 49503

Translated from the Dutch edition *Numeri: Een praktische bijbelverklaring*, part of the Tekst en Toelichting series. © Uitgersmaatschappij J. H. Kok—Kampen, 1985.

Library of Congress Cataloging-in-Publication Data:

Maarsingh, B.
　Numbers: a practical commentary.

　(Text and interpretation)
　Translation of: Numeri.
　1. Bible. O.T. Numbers—Commentaries. I. Title.
II. Series.
BS1265.3.M3313　1987　　222'.14077　　86-29263

ISBN 0-8028-0104-8

CONTENTS

TRANSLATOR'S PREFACE

In translating this volume from the Dutch original, I have consistently tried to make it both readable and readily useful, for the pastor as well as for the layperson.

Bible quotations are taken from the Revised Standard Version, except where the author's own translation was closer in letter and spirit to another version. In those cases, I followed the appropriate version—New International, New English, or occasionally other versions—and indicated this in the text. In some instances, where none of the common English versions captured the author's intent, I made a note to that effect in the text.

It is my earnest wish that users of this commentary may derive as much pleasure and instruction from reading it as I did in translating it.

—John Vriend

INTRODUCTION

I. TERMS USED IN THE COMMENTARY

In preparing this commentary I worked from my own translation of the Hebrew. In this process it proved necessary to consult the text of the Samaritan Pentateuch and the other ancient translations regularly, including the Greek version (the Septuagint), which is at times markedly divergent from the Hebrew text, and the various Aramaic versions—the so-called Targums—among which the Targum Pseudo-Jonathan gets the most attention (his Targum has substantial differences from the Hebrew text, including many long digressions, which are sometimes very worthwhile but in some cases sound strange and even fantastic). I also consulted Jerome's Latin translation, the Vulgate, which is generally fine but often deviates somewhat from the original. In the course of consulting these texts I encountered the difficulties the ancients already struggled with, and I profited from the solutions they devised.

I commonly refer to the people as "all the Israelites" and to the official representation of all as "the congregation." Its large subdivisions are the twelve tribes whose names go back to the sons of Jacob. When I mention the descendants of Levi alongside the other tribes, I refer to them as "Levites"; when I refer to the members within this tribe, I distinguish between the priests on the one hand and all others on the other hand, calling the latter "levites." I refer to the largest subdivisions of the tribes as "clans" (what the RSV refers to as "families"). The clans in turn are composed of "families" (what the RSV refers to as "fathers' houses"). The smallest unit is the family.

I usually refer to the central sanctuary as "the tent of meeting," because the Hebrew word behind it implies a specific time and a specific place at which the people came together: a time and place of meeting God and one another. Sometimes I use another designation—"the tabernacle of the testimony" (e.g., in my commentary on Num. 1:50)—in which case we

1

have to take the word "testimony" as a designation of the rules that the covenant between the Lord and Israel imposed on the people. Whether the phrase "dwelling place" refers to the entire sanctuary or only a part of it depends on the context.

Common translations of words having to do with sacrifices are not as a rule very satisfactory, often failing to reproduce the specific intent of the various sacrifices. On the basis of research I undertook in connection with a commentary on Leviticus, I made bold to replace most of these terms. Only the terms "sin offering" and "guilt offering" clearly indicate the purpose of these respective offerings; I have changed the names of the other sacrifices. The burnt offering that is totally consumed on the altar is the sign of the acknowledgment of God's majesty and is a visible expression of total surrender, which led me to refer to is as an "offering to God's majesty." The same thing can be said of the food or cereal offering, which is often mentioned in one breath with the offering to God's majesty. It was much less costly, but it too indicated that the person making the offering was bowing down before the high God. Outside the cultic sphere, the term refers to the tribute a vassal owed his overlord; hence, I refer to it as a "homage offering." Most likely the drink offering had a similar intent, serving as a sign of respect, of a person returning something to God.

The terms "sacrificial offering" and "peace offering" derive from three Hebrew words designating offerings that involve placing the blood and fat of a sacrificial animal on the altar, giving a small predetermined portion of the animal to the priest, and giving very much the largest portion of the animal to the sacrificer and his family. This was the way one experienced fellowship with God and with other members of the congregation, which is why I speak of communal offerings.

The so-called "fire offering" probably had nothing to do with fire. We do not know what the word does mean, and so I adopted the term "special offering" for lack of a better one. In connection with these special offerings before the Lord, we often encounter the phrase "a pleasing odor." The Hebrew, however, tends to point more in the direction of "rest" and so I have translated the phrase as "a soothing odor."

II. THE CONTENT

The name of the fourth book of the Bible is not very meaningful and certainly not very applicable to the whole. In any case, it tends to turn off the interest of the beginning reader. From the Greek translation and through the Latin, the name came into our language as *Numbers*, but this name applies to only a small part of the book—to the numbering of the fighting men and the census of the Levites; to the listing of the gifts given to the sanctuary and the offerings prescribed for the festivities; to the marches that were made and the stops along the way where the people stayed overnight or longer; and to a few other scattered figures.

By far the larger part of Numbers contains material of a very different nature, however. One finds in it the various prescriptions for the cult in the sanctuary covering the duties and the rights of the servants in the sanctuary as well as the conditions the people had to meet in order to have access to the holy assembly. The book also addresses the broad area of jurisprudence. Regarding capital crimes the law was severe, but it did allow that those who committed accidental homicide might save their lives by fleeing to a place of refuge. No one who committed theft in any form was allowed to escape punishment, however; Israelite law first demanded restitution of that which was stolen. In the matter of inheritance rights, care was taken to protect the interests of both individual female heirs and members of the community to which the female heirs belonged. In the context of marriage, rules were laid down to protect the lawful rights of the husband, but there was a heavier emphasis on the protection of the woman when she was unjustly suspected of infidelity. Vows once made had to be kept. When a girl living at home or a married woman made a vow, she was bound by the decision of the man who had authority over her. Clear rules were instituted for the special kind of vow taken by the Nazirites. Thus the book of Numbers covers the whole of life: the cult, society as a whole, the family, and the individual.

It's interesting to note what Leviticus has to say on the same subjects. There are many connections between the two books, as there are between Numbers and the second part of Exodus.

In addition to rules and prescriptions, Numbers contains pieces of the history of the wilderness period. The name by which Jews generally refer to the book is much more graphic. Using a phrase from the first line, they call it "In the wilderness." Numbers begins in the wilderness and ends in the fields of Moab north of the Dead Sea. In between these two points stretches a history of thirty-eight years, beginning with a campaign that ended in failure, as the people, filled with unbelief and distrust, expressed a desire to return to Egypt. Next followed the long period of wanderings, during which it was in all likelihood always possible to fall back on Kadesh-barnea. We get to hear and see in a few flashes rebellious mutterings, fists clenched and raised up, and resulting setbacks that caused thousands to lose their lives. Finally, after an entire generation had passed from the scene, the people arrived at the gate of the promised land a second time—not from the south this time but by way of Moab over against Jericho, skirting around Edom. Victory over two kings in Trans-Jordan gave the people courage for the future. In the end, though, even more decisive events took place. The king of Moab hired the soothsayer-prophet Balaam in an attempt to render the people powerless and to put a curse on them. However, at Peor only blessings came out of the man's mouth. Evidence of the name Balaam that has turned up in diggings at Tell Deir Alla suggests that this man must have made a strong impression on later generations. Jewish tradition tells us that his name was linked with idolatry occurring just before the invasion of the promised land. Also connected with this was the rebuke of the Midianites, a nomadic people apparently allied with Moab. In all these historical accounts we are reminded of the first part of Exodus.

III. THE PLACE OF MOSES

What is the place or role of Moses in the book of Numbers? In a few places he is pictured as a leader who possessed real authority. He was addressed as such by Joshua ("My lord, Moses," 11:28) and by his brother Aaron (12:11). Similarly, the Gadites and Reubenites and the men of Gilead in call him "my lord" (32:35; 36:2). And that he was, called to this unusually heavy task by God himself.

But this leadership role did not mean that he was called to rule over the people, as he was accused of doing (16:13). Indeed, the opposite was true: this leader was a servant. This was pointed out most dramatically during the darkest periods of Israel's sojourn in the wilderness. When the Israelites began to put themselves in opposition to God so truculently that God decided to wipe them all out in judgment, it was the man who had suffered most under their indictments that proceeded to take up the cudgels for them. He was ready to bear the suffering that the guilty had brought upon themselves if necessary. As is evident from Ps. 100:23, this side of Moses' character remained a living memory for centuries. Against this background, words such as those recorded in 16:15 and 20:10-11 are appalling. But it is characteristic of the Bible to show us the whole person—failures included.

In most instances, however, he came forward and acted as the great prophet. Over and over we hear such expressions as "the Lord spoke to Moses," "the Lord commanded Moses," and "according to the word of the Lord." In the book of Numbers alone these expressions, almost always addressed to Moses, occur 139 times. A particularly important statement in 12:6-8 says two things about the fact Moses was chosen to convey the words of God to the people. First there is the negative point that the Lord used neither a vision during the day nor a dream at night to address this prophet, though he had used these devices to speak to other men of God. Second is the positive point that there was a special relationship between God and Moses that involved direct contact.

The dialogue between the high God and puny man here was direct, personal, face-to-face. That is the very highest thing that can be said. This servant of God was even deemed worthy of seeing God's form. The same thing is said in Exodus 33:23, though this text is more reserved and only speaks of his seeing God's "back." So Moses was valued above all others. There is only One of whom we can say more—Jesus Christ—but he is himself the Word, one with the Father.

IV. THE FINAL REDACTION

The book of Numbers is so dominated by Moses that it is typically referred to as the fourth of the "five books of Moses," the others being Genesis, Exodus, Leviticus, and Deuteronomy. Likewise, the Old Testament is commonly divided into the Law, the Prophets, and the Writings, and the later scriptures often equate Moses with the Law—hence the New Testament habit of saying "Moses says." It is a question, however, whether this warrants the conclusion that Moses actually wrote the first five books of the Bible. Concerning Numbers, we can venture a few points in this regard.

A large part of the book presupposes the life in the wilderness and reproduces the events that took place there during this period. The people lived in tents, stayed at a given place for a given period of time, broke camp, and went on. In the middle of the camp stood the "tent of meeting" (though some passages seem to suggest that it was set up outside the camp). This sanctuary was the place where the Lord wanted to meet his people. Continual concern over adequate food and drink marked life in the wilderness. In that context there are repeated references to springs and to manna.

Conflict with nomadic tribes was, predictably, another feature of life in the wilderness. On the other hand, certain parts of the book presuppose the normal life of cattle raisers and farmers. It was their large livestock holdings that made it attractive for Gad and Reuben to remain in Trans-Jordan. The religious festivals of Israel most probably originated in agricultural life: the Feast of Unleavened Bread in the barley harvest, the Feast of Weeks in the wheat harvest, and the Feast of Booths in the fruit harvest. As a rule, wine was used for drink offerings. Further, there are many references to villages and cities. A special feature is the designation of certain cities for the levites. Mention is also made of cities of refuge, which suggests a well-developed society. It could easily be the case that the so-called second Passover in 9:1-14 presupposes the centralization of the cult at the time of King Josiah, who ruled from 639 to 603 B.C., for that is when the problems of distance arise. But the text itself proceeds from the assumption that these problems already existed in the wilderness period. This, in turn, assumes that the tribes were spread over a large area in the years of their wanderings.

From 33:2 we know that Moses himself put down in writing the list of starting places. Further, 21:14-15 contains the quotation from the "Book of the Wars of the Lord," regrettably lost now. Apparently this book told of military actions in close connection with religion. Did it report battles in the wilderness, or was the subject the military conquest of the promised land? Must we perhaps date the book in the time of the kings? Another lost work, the "Book of the Upright" mentioned in Joshua 10:13 and 2 Samuel 1:18, goes back in any case to the time of the kings. Whatever the case, the passage in Numbers based on the Book of the Wars of the Lord is of course more recent than the lost document from antiquity. This brings us to the premise that more sources of this sort may have been used. Till now it has been impossible to say precisely what these might have been. Many a theory has been devised, not one of which is entirely satisfactory. Perhaps some progress can be made by observing how many times the divine oracle occurs and looking to see whether some system is being followed. It is striking, for instance, that the numbers three, four, and seven play an important role (see Caspar J. Labuschagne, "The Pattern of the Divine Speech Formulas in the Pentateuch," *Vetus Testamentum* 32 [1982]: 286-96).

It must have taken centuries before all the available data were assembled into the book we now have before us. The person or persons who completed this great work resided in Canaan proper, as is evident from the fact that when they speak of Trans-Jordan they always mean the territory east of the river. Those who speak about the same area from an eastern vantage point always add the words "eastern" or "where the sun rises."

We may get a hint as to when the final redaction of the book was made by considering the dating systems used—in this case, the Babylonian calendar. This calendar fixes the New Year in the spring of the year. The Israelite calendar, however, was calculated from a point in the fall of the year—in keeping with a farmer's calendar from Gezer, which goes back to the tenth century B.C. In all likelihood it was during the final years of the period of the kings that the change from the fall to the spring was made, so it must have been some time after this that the final redaction of Numbers was completed. Some scholars, on the basis of papyri found at Elephantine in Egypt (where there was a Jewish military colony in the fifth century B.C.), wish to go farther and set the date at 419 B.C.

In any event, the evidence is that this one document contains data from different times. What they all have in common is a phrase that can be translated literally as "by the hand of Moses"—that is, by his mediation, on his authority, according to the rules that God laid down. All the data—those of the period in the wilderness, those of the conquest, those of later times—are covered by the authority of this leader-mediator-prophet. They breathe his spirit, no matter when they were written down. All that matters is that they were inspired by the same Spirit who governed Moses.

V. BIBLIOGRAPHY

Budd, Philip J. *Numbers*. Word Biblical Commentary, vol. 5. Waco, Tex.: Word Books, 1984.

Coats, George. *Rebellion in the Wilderness: The Murmuring Motif in the Wilderness Traditions of the Old Testament*. Nashville: Abingdon Press, 1968.

Cross, F. M. *Canaanite Myth and Hebrew Epic: Essays in the History of the Religion of Israel*. Cambridge, Mass.: Harvard University Press, 1974.

De Vaux, Roland. *Ancient Israel*. Translated by J. McHugh. London: Darton, Longman & Todd, 1961. Rpt., New York: McGraw-Hill, 1965.

Gray, G. B. *A Critical and Exegetical Commentary on Numbers*. The International Critical Commentary, 1903. Rpt., Edinburgh: T. & T. Clark, 1976.

Levine, B. A. *In the Presence of the Lord: A Study of Cult and Some Cultic Terms in Ancient Israel*. Leiden: E. J. Brill, 1974.

Milgrom, Jacob. *Studies in Levitical Terminology*. Vol. 1. Berkeley and Los Angeles: University of California Press, 1970.

Noth, Martin. *Numbers: A Commentary*. Old Testament Library. Translated by J. D. Martin. Philadelphia: Westminster Press, 1968.

Snaith, Norman H. *Leviticus and Numbers*. New Century Bible. London: Thomas Nelson, 1969. Rpt., London: Marshall, Morgan & Scott, 1977.

Sturdy, J. *Numbers*. Cambridge Bible Commentary. Cambridge: Cambridge University Press, 1972.

Wenham, Gordon J. *Numbers*. Tyndale Old Testament Commentaries. Downers Grove, Ill.: InterVarsity Press, 1981.

COMMENTARY ON NUMBERS

THE NUMBERING OF THE TRIBES 1:1-19

Verse one refers to the exodus from Egypt, which must have taken place around 1225 B.C., at a time when that great kingdom was threatened from different directions. From the data provided in Exodus and Numbers we may deduce the following pattern of events:

1. The exodus on the fifteenth day of the first month of the first year (Exod. 12:6, 18; Num. 33:2)
2. The arrival at Sinai on the same day of the third month of the first year (Exod. 19:1)
3. The setting up of the tent on the first day of the first month of the second year (Exod. 40:2, 17)
4. The command to number the people on the first day of the second month of the second year (Num. 1:1)
5. The departure from the Sinai area on the twentieth day of the second month of the second year (Num. 10:11)

The events reported in Leviticus must have taken place in the first month of the second year, and the events reported in Numbers 1:1–10:10 in the next twenty days.

According to Numbers 1:1, the Lord spoke to Moses in the "tent of meeting," while further on in the chapter there is recurrent reference to the "tabernacle of the testimony"; both are references to the same portable sanctuary. References to the tent of meeting emphasize the appointed place where God and the people could find each other; references to the tabernacle of the testimony emphasize the rules Israel had to adhere to in order to keep their covenant with the Lord intact. In both instances, it was God who determined whether he would continue to dwell among his own as the God of the covenant, and it was in this sanctuary that he involved his servant Moses in disclosing his will to the people. In this section the concern is with the numbering, or census taking, which is described at length in verses 20-46.

The work of taking the census was not done by Moses alone; he was assisted by Aaron and twelve representatives of the tribes, as is evident in verse 16. The first of the titles used to describe those whose office consisted in calling the popular assembly together can be translated as "conveners"; it can also be translated "the convened," to highlight the fact that they were chosen from the whole community. In either case, they were special people. The second title is related to the verb "to raise up," or "to elevate," and signifies that they were raised up by God or the people or both to a position above the others, to become leaders in Israel. The third title is a word simply meaning "head," though here it refers to someone with a high rank. Precisely the same word served to designate numbers of the high nobility under the emperor of Ethiopia.

A word needs to be said about the names used in this passage. The meaning of some of them remains uncertain. A few are neutral in content. Many contain a divine name, such as "El" ("God") and "Shaddai" ("Almighty"). Parts of a name— Ahi ("my brother") and Ammi ("my relation")—may also contain references to God (see v. 12). Striking, however, is the total absence of the name of Israel's God, YHWH, reproduced in the RSV by the word "LORD." Nobody knows how the sacred name was pronounced in ancient Israel; now we must simply make do with the best possible substitute. One runs into personal names that contain the divine name—"Jo" or "Jeho" when it comes first and "Yah" or "Yahu" when it comes last—especially in the time of the kings. Examples include Johanan or Jehohanan (= "the Lord is gracious") and Hananiah (= "gracious is the Lord"). The fact that the true Israelite name for God occurs in none of the twenty-four names listed here has led some scholars to assign a late date to the composition of this list—during or after the exile. It seems to me much more likely that it implies a very ancient date, that it must have been composed during or before the wilderness period.

THE NUMBERS 1:20-47

The people as a unit are called "Israel" or "the congregation" or "the assembly of the people." This larger unit was subdivided into tribes. The tribe of Levi was not included in the numbering, because it was exempt from military service. The final count is still twelve tribes, however, because the tribe of

Joseph was split into Ephraim and Manasseh. Each tribe comprised smaller units that we cannot describe with precision but that can roughly be called "clans" (what the RSV refers to as "families"). The clan was composed of families (what the RSV refers to as "fathers' houses") who had a sense of common ancestry. The family consisted of individuals, referred to in the Hebrew text with the word "skulls," which is reproduced in the RSV as "head by head."

It appears that prior to the time of which the text is speaking it had not been possible to assemble a clear, complete, and comprehensive record of the many tribes, clans, families, and individuals in the nation of Israel. At this point, however, God gave Moses, along with his brother Aaron and twelve leading men from among the people, the task of taking a census of all the tribes. The practical reason for taking this census was to register all the able-bodied men over the age of twenty for military service. The point is made in the text that this command came not from a human being (as in 2 Sam. 24)—not even from so great a historical figure as Moses; rather, it came from God himself, and therefore had to be a good undertaking. The census spoken of here in chapter 1 took place after the events at Mount Sinai; a second census referred to in chapter 26 occurred thirty-eight years later. The difference in time explains the difference in the numbers.

There has been much discussion of the numbers. Some scholars understand the numbers literally, accepting as true the report that about a year after the exodus there were 603,550 able-bodied men trekking through the wilderness, and that just before the entry the number stood at 601,730. But to determine the size of the people as a whole, we would have to multiply that number by at least four (to include the women and children)—which would bring the total to approximately two and a half million, a number that seems to many quite impossible. But then how do we proceed? We might look to the symbolic use in Scripture of such numbers as seven, twelve, forty, a hundred, a thousand, and ten thousand. Perhaps they are being used as we sometimes use numbers in English, saying "I must have said it a hundred times" when we mean simply "very often." But if that's what is happening here, why aren't round numbers used? Such problems have led scholars to look in other directions.

In Hebrew there are no signs for numerals; letters are used

instead. The first letter of the alphabet is 1, the second 2, the third 3, and so on. Using this formula, one can assign numerical values to words and phrases. It is interesting to note that the Hebrew phrase "sons of Israel" has a numerical value of 603—the first three numbers of the census figure 603,550. But then what do we do with the remaining 550?

Other scholars seek an explanation by focusing on the word for "thousand." Originally, this word was the sign for the head of an ox; then it came to signify the whole ox; later it was used to refer to a herd of cattle; later still it was used to refer to a number of animals or people; and finally it came to signify a thousand. If we were to understand "thousand" to mean "group," then when we read that "the number of the tribe of Reuben was forty-six thousand five hundred" (v. 21) we might understand it to mean that the tribe comprised forty-six groups which together came to five hundred people. But this, too, leads to difficulties.

Other scholars suggest that the term translated as "thousand" simply has some other unknown numerical value—that $46,500 = 46x + 500$. Still others have attempted to establish a connection between the numbers and the astral world. But however we turn or twist the problem, we are faced with very high numbers, the significance of which remains obscure to us.

I myself believe that these high numbers serve to underscore how a group of people that was insignificant at the beginning grew to be a multitude that could be compared with the stars of heaven and the sand on the seashore. God's promise to the patriarchs was already being realized in the wilderness, and the fabulous figures point to the fact.

Whatever the meaning of the numbers, a closer scrutiny yields many surprises. We find, for example, that the tribe of Simeon, which later disappeared entirely, was at this point much larger than the powerful tribe of Ephraim had been in the time of the kings. We find that the tribe of Dan was one of the largest, whereas Judges 17 and 18 tells us that at that time it had contained only six hundred armed men. We also find that the tribe of Judah was already playing the most important role in the wilderness period.

THE TRIBE OF LEVI 1:48-54

Because they had a special task, the Levites were not counted in the general numbering. Although their work was also called "military service," they did not bear arms. Their service was closely connected with the sanctuary. In this passage, the sanctuary is not called "the tent of meeting" but "the tabernacle of the testimony"—*testimony* referring to the rules of the covenant between God and the people. The mission of the Levites was threefold. When the sanctuary was set up, it was their duty as helpers of the priests to provide for the administration of worship. When the people moved on, it was their task to break down the tent and later to set it up again. And every time the people camped in a new place, the Levites had to set up their tents around the sanctuary in order to provide a ring of protection. The other Israelites occupied their own designated places in the plan of settlement, each tribe in a separate section behind its own standard, but it was the task of the Levites to mount a guard around the tabernacle of the testimony. That, too, was a kind of military service, but it was directed inward—to prevent any unauthorized person from coming too close. Such an act could provoke an outburst of wrath from God against the people as a whole. For that reason an extremely severe punishment was laid down in law against breaking through the boundaries set by the holiness of God: death. Our God is a consuming fire.

POSITIONING THE TRIBES 2:1-34

The word "standard" in verse 2 has a double meaning, denoting both the banner around which a given tribe gathered and the tribe itself. The word "ensign" in verse 2 really means "sign." Each tribe had its own standard; each family had its own ensign.

Chapter 2 outlines the positioning of the different tribes and gives instructions concerning the formations in which they had to assemble when they broke camp and responded to the order to go forward. The order of the tribes here is not quite identical with that in chapter 1, but the names of the leaders are exactly the same, as are the sizes of the tribes, so this section appropriately follows the numbering of the people as a whole.

The camp was set up in a clear pattern. The tent of meeting was central and was always set up to face the east. Around it the tents of the priests and levites were arranged as a protective wall. Around this central campground, in a wide circle, were the divisions of the other tribes. The priests and the levites settled down in specific assigned locations as did the other tribes. The most important side was the east, then the south, then the west, and finally the north.

In considering the positioning of the tribes, we should note not only the place given to each but also the fact that their ranking is related to the status of the women from whom they descended. Information about the four women—the sisters Leah and Rachel and the concubines Zilpah and Bilhah—can be found in the story of the patriarch Jacob in Genesis 29:31–30:24 and 35:18. The children of Leah and Rachel had the most status (it is possible that those of Leah had slightly more status than those of Rachel inasmuch as Leah was the elder of the two). The children of the concubines had a decidedly lower rank than those of the primary wives.

The tribe of Judah, together with the tribes of Judah's two full brothers Issachar and Zebulun (all three of whom were sons of Leah), occupied the most important location, directly facing the entrance of the tent of meeting. This is remarkable: it was not the eldest son, Reuben, who occupied the first place; nor was it the second son, Simeon; nor was it even the third son, Levi (whose tribe belonged to the sanctuary, of course). It was the fourth son, Judah, who was designated to be the first. Together, the tribes of Judah, Issachar, and Zebulun are said to have contained 186,400 able-bodied fighting men, by far the largest military force among the Israelites; and of these three, Judah itself was the largest.

In second place was Leah's eldest son, Reuben, together with his full brother Simeon and his half-brother Gad, a son of Leah's slave woman, Zilpah. Though the oldest son, Reuben was not granted the position of the first-born. But neither was he shoved to the side; he retained an important place as second in rank. Numbering a total of 151,450 able-bodied fighting men, these three tribes constituted a force only slightly less than that of the group to the north.

In third place were the tribes of Joseph and Benjamin, descendants of Rachel; the tribe of Joseph was split into the tribes of Ephraim and Manasseh. As a result of God's elective actions, two remarkable changes occurred in these tribes: (1) Ephraim and Manasseh, the children of Joseph, took precedence over the descendants of their ancestor's uncle Benjamin, and (2) Manasseh, the oldest son, occupied second place rather than first. The leadership of the three tribes fell to the youngest, Ephraim. Numbering 108,100 able-bodied fighting men, these three tribes formed the least powerful military force— startling in light of the greatness and power of Ephraim in the time of the kings!

The remaining three tribes were Dan, Asher, and Naphtali, which camped on the north side. Dan, son of Bilhah, Rachel's slave, was their leader. As descendants of concubines (Asher was a son of Zilpah, and Naphtali was a son of Bilhah), the three tribes naturally had a lower rank. Numbering 157,600 able-bodied men, they constituted a somewhat larger force than did the Reuben group.

When the entire camp was set up, the tent of meeting was located in the middle, with the tribe of Levi encamped closely around it. The Egyptians characteristically placed the tent of the king, his generals, and officers at the center of a large army camp, but for the Israelites another tent was central: the sanctuary in which it pleased God to dwell among his people. From him proceeds the power to save and to defend, and from this tent in the middle he made known his ever-saving will.

When God would give the command that his people must resume the march, his presence among them would show up anew. The long line of onward-marching Israelites would unwind again—first the powerful Judah group, then the Reuben group, then the tent of meeting with the Levi group; then the Ephraim group, and finally the Dan group. So always, at rest or in motion, the tent, the sign of God's presence, would remain in the middle. If it pleased him thus to march with his people, one can say with conviction: God-with-us!

Whether we are in camp or on the march, the important thing is the awesome fact that God's grace is with us. This God is our God, always and forever.

PRIESTS AND LEVITES 3:1-13

Verses 1-4 record the names of the descendants of Aaron at the time the Lord spoke to Moses on Mount Sinai. Of the four sons, two died (Lev. 10:1-2) because they offered unauthorized fire before the Lord and thus blocked the progress of worship. Since neither of them had sons of his own, the priestly service was transferred to the younger brothers, who subsequently carried out the work under the supervision of their father. In the relationship with God every form of neglect invites severe judgment. At stake is the majesty of that which is holy.

In verse 5 and following we read that God issued a series of new commands to Moses. An earlier focus on the priests is now transferred to the levites, whose task it was to serve. They were joined to the priests in order to assume responsibility for certain kinds of priestly work and tasks that belonged to the community as a whole. Their labor was in the domain of the holy dwelling (vv. 7-8; to underscore the specificity of their work, v. 8 repeats what is said in v. 7). In this capacity they were, in the full sense of the word, people *given* by the Lord to the priests as substitutes for the people as a whole. Meanwhile, the priestly work itself was reserved for Aaron and his sons. Verse 10b repeats the warning to the unauthorized. The sacred space remained screened off, for God is holy.

In verses 11-13 we find the background of God's action in relation to the tribe of Levi, which has to do with the firstborn. The power of a people lies in the birth of its progeny, and so a great value was placed on the first child to be born—a value so great, in fact, that in many nations the eldest son was sacrificed to the gods. Verse 13 refers to the fact that the Lord broke the power of Egypt by killing all the first-born. From that point on, he regarded every first-born in Israel as his own—the first-born of cattle as well as of the people. He directed that the first-born of clean (i.e., unblemished) cattle were to be offered on the altar; the first-born of unclean (i.e., blemished) cattle were either replaced with clean animals for sacrifice or they were simply killed. In Israel the first-born of the people were never sacrificed. They were either "redeemed" or "replaced" in a manner analogous to the procedure for the animals. Specifically, the tribe of the Levites served as substitute first-born for all of the Israelite people, and they were sacrificed by being placed totally at the disposal of the Lord.

THE CLANS OF LEVI 3:14-39

Since priests and levites did not render military service in the same fashion as the members of the other tribes, they were numbered separately from the others. It is specified that the count was to include all the male members of the tribe a month old or older—indicating that a child of that age was obviously regarded as sufficiently viable. The registration included the name, the family lineage, the clan, and the tribe.

This passage offers a clear overview of the clans and families: their names, their leaders, their size, their location in relation to the sanctuary, and their task. There were three main clans: the Gershonites, the Kohathites, and the Merarites. The relative status of these clans is once again indicated by the positions of their encampments. The most important location was the one on the east side, facing the entrance of the tent of meeting, and it was here that the priestly division camped— Aaron and his sons, who had charge over the rites performed within the sanctuary (v. 38). Although Moses was not a priest, he also had a place by the entrance of the tent. It should be noted that he was a descendant of Levi and that he sometimes acted in a priestly capacity. The priests descended, via Amram, from the Kohathites, and so this clan was accorded the next most important position, on the south side. The descendants of Gershon camped on the west side, and the Merarites camped on the north side.

As to the names of the leaders, it may be noted that five out of six contain the divine name "El," whereas the sixth name, Abihail (v. 35), might contain a reference to deity in the fragment "Abi" (= "my father"). The name YHWH does not occur in any of them—a sign perhaps, of the great antiquity of the list?

Adding the numbers up, we come to a final figure of 22,300. Verse 39, however, says 22,000. The most plausible explanation of this discrepancy is that at some point a scribe dropped out one Hebrew letter "l" in copying verse 28. If this letter were inserted, the number would be 8,300 rather than 8,600, and the 22,000 figure would be correct.

The tasks that the four different groups of Levites had to perform depended on the places in which they camped.

First of all, the priests on the east side worked on behalf of the people as a whole in the sanctuary. They were even permitted to enter the sacred spaces; once a year, by God's special grace, the high priest was permitted to enter the Most Holy Place (Lev. 16). They were allowed to see and to touch the holy articles, and when the people broke camp to journey further it was their responsibility to wrap these objects in cloths. In the regular ministry of worship they used all the holy utensils to perform the rites.

The Kohathites were assigned to take care of such holy objects as the ark, the table for the showbread, the lampstand, the altar of incense, the curtain, and the "altars" (the plural probably implies a reference to the altar in the forecourt).

The Gershonites were assigned to take care of the lighter parts of the sanctuary, such as the coverings, curtains, and tent ropes—in short all that was made of animal skins or woven fabrics (materials less holy that those cared for by the Kohathites).

The remaining materials—the boards, the beams, the posts, the bases, the tent pegs, and the ropes—fell under the responsibility of the Merarites. They clearly had the heaviest work to do of any of the clans of Levi when the sanctuary was to be moved.

In verse 32 we read that Eleazar the son of Aaron was given chief responsibility for supervising all levites who performed work in or around the sanctuary. In effect he was given the ultimate charge to stand guard over the holiness of the tent.

THE FIRST-BORN AND THE LEVITES 3:40-51

Verses 40-43 connect with verses 11-13, in which mention is also made of levites as substitutes for the first-born. The information is presented somewhat differently, and some new points are made about the cattle. The total count of the first-born in Israel turns out to be 22,273. By taking the levites in their stead, the Lord makes them his special possession. The addition of the phrase "I am the Lord" (v. 41; cf. v. 45) underscores his claim on them.

In part, verses 44-51 constitute a literal repetition of verses 40-43. Since there are 22,273 first-born in Israel, and 22,000 Levites, there arises the difficulty of what to do with the "surplus" of 273. The Lord commands that they be redeemed by paying a sum of money—five shekels apiece. In all, that adds up to 1,365 shekels from the first-born.

Inasmuch as the Lord had "given" the levites to the priests, this amount properly belonged to Aaron and his sons. The silver was weighed in terms of the sanctuary shekel. We know of other shekels as well: those of the merchants (Gen. 23:16) and those of the palace (2 Sam. 14:26). We do not know the difference in weight between them, nor do we know the precise weight of the sanctuary shekel, but it was approximately two-fifths of an ounce (see the note on v. 47 in the NIV).

The reference to the cattle is striking. In verse 41 we read that the cattle of the Levites were to substitute for the first-born among the cattle of the Israelites, just as the Levites themselves were to substitute for the first-born of the Israelites. But verse 45 says that the cattle of the Levites were to take the place of *their* cattle. Whose cattle? Those of all the Israelites? That would have been a lot. Or is the reference to the cattle of the first-born? Could it be that just as the Levites were to take the place of the first-born, so the cattle of the Levites take the place of the cattle of the first-born? If we switch the words "first-born" and "cattle" in verse 41, we would get the same result: the cattle of every first-born. It is an attractive solution. On the other hand, it is possible that this command was in force only once. In chapter 18 the assumption is that every first-born among the people would be redeemed with money and that every first-born animal would be sacrificed or redeemed or simply killed (cf. Exod. 13:13). The Levites, however, remained completely at the Lord's disposal.

THE TASKS OF THE LEVITES 4:1-49

Chapter 4 takes the data of chapter 3 and works them out in detail. In the process the text not only mentions a large number of parts and articles of the tent of meeting but also describes precisely the coverings with which each object had to be covered, what color each covering had to be, and how much covering was needed in each instance.

Two words are used repeatedly in connection with the Levites that call for comment—namely, "task" and "load" [NEB]. Since the subject of this chapter is principally the breaking up of the camp, the word "task" refers not to work done in connection with the cult or to the protection of the tent against intruders but to the work of taking apart and rebuilding the sanctuary. The word "load," which is derived from the verb "to carry," refers to picking up, carrying, and transporting everything that belonged to the tent. The notion of "military service" may have been closely associated with battle in the minds of other Israelites, but to the Levites it meant all labor in and around the sanctuary.

When at the command of God the people broke camp, the

first to go to work at the tent were the priests. They had to see to it that the holy articles were wrapped in certain coverings and readied for transport by inserting poles or placing them in a carrying frame (4:6, 8, 10). This concerned the ark first of all—the ark of the testimony, so named because it contained the rules of the covenant, the ten commandments. Next came the table of the showbread, literally called the table of the Presence (4:7). Next to be readied was the golden lampstand and its accessories (4:7, 10); then the little golden altar (4:11); and finally, the big altar in the forecourt. The Samaritan text and the Septuagint add to this list the bronze laver. In the nature of the case, all the accessories belonging to these holy objects must have been included. Verse 16 informs us that Eleazar continued to be personally responsible for a few things himself.

After all the holy objects had been wrapped up and covered, the Kohathites were allowed to come in to lift everything off the ground, to carry and transport it—under the supervision of Eleazar, son of Aaron. A parenthesis in verses 17-20 gives the reason the priests had to act with such care and caution. They, and they alone, had access to the holy things. It was their duty to see that no unauthorized person came too near. The levites were counted among these unauthorized persons. They too had to remain outside the domain of the holy, had to avoid touching anything that was holy. Even to look at a holy object only for a moment with the naked eye would mean death. By wrapping all the holy articles in cloths, the priests were protecting the Kohathites from ruin. They were assigned the area in which they could safely position themselves and only then given permission to transport their sacred load.

Next the Gershonites would take responsibility for their share of the sanctuary—all the articles that were easy to carry, such as curtains, screens, coverings, and tent ropes. They did their work under the supervision of Ithamar, the other son of Aaron.

Finally the Merarites would come on the scene. Their task was to carry the heavy parts of the tent—also under Ithamar's supervision.

These details point out the significant differences between the priests and the other descendants of Levi, and between the Levites and the other tribes. It was a consistently applied hierarchy that became ever more visible in the later history of the Jews.

In verses 34-49 we find an account of the census to which the Levites had to submit. In this instance, the focus of interest is not, as in the preceding chapter, on the male members of the tribe but on those who are permitted to render service.

According to verse 35, the Levites served from age 30 to 50. Numbers 8:24-25 indicates that they served from age 25 to 50. According to 1 Chronicles 20:24, 2 Chronicles 31:17, and Ezra 3:8, the Levites began to serve at age 20. The Septuagint translation of verse 35 has 25 instead of 30 as the starting age. What is the meaning of these variations? Did the rule depend on circumstances? Did it depend on the number of cult servants available? Should we regard the first five years as a training period, a kind of prior practice with an eye to mastering the necessary precision? Or did the heavy responsibility require greater age? We know that a large part of the work of the Levites consisted in the religious training of the people. In view of the fact that in ancient times people matured more rapidly than they do today, one would already be fairly old at 20, not to mention 25 or 30.

The census was done by the familiar rules, listing clan, family, and name. The Kohathites were numbered at 2,750, the Gershonites at 2,630, and the Merarites at 3,200, for a total of 8,580. Comparing these figures with those of Numbers 3, we note that fewer than half but more than a third of the males were in service.

THE PURITY OF THE CAMP 5:1-4

The heart of the matter is presented in verse 3: "where I dwell among them" [NIV]. God's holy presence among his people can tolerate no impurity. The text mentions three forms of impurity. The first is extensively discussed in Leviticus 13 and 14 and is usually translated "leprosy." It is very much the question, however, whether the reference is really to what we now know as Hansen's Disease. In any case, here, as in Leviticus, the people were instructed to send everyone suffering from this dreaded disease out of the camp. The second form of impurity is treated in Leviticus 15 under the term "discharge." There it is said that those individuals who have a discharge are to be considered unclean for seven days, though they need not be sent out of the camp. In this regard, Numbers 5:1-4 is much more strict. The same is true of its instructions concerning a person who has become unclean by contact with a dead body. According to Numbers 19, such an individual remains unclean for seven days but is not shut out from the community. Numbers 5 does demand expulsion of such an individual, though—an extremely severe measure that puts a very heavy emphasis on God's unapproachable holiness. In light of such restrictions, it becomes even more miraculous that he would be willing to continue to dwell in the midst of his people.

MAKING REPARATION 5:5-10

The issue dealt with in Numbers 5:1-8 is also treated in much greater detail in Leviticus 6:1-7, which discusses several cases of dereliction in matters of personal property. The expression "sins that men commit" in Numbers 5:6 may be understood to mean not only sin committed by a human being but also sin committed against a human being, though of the two meanings I prefer the latter. From what follows it is clear that the text deals with sin for which a person has to make reparation, which indicates that the offense being discussed involves property. The man or woman in question has taken something from another, has committed a theft, has fraudulently taken or kept goods belonging to another. Therefore, the guilty individual owes a debt to the injured neighbor, having been unfaithful to that neighbor. And the guilty person owes a debt to God as well, since any wrong we commit against a fellow human being has an immediate effect on our relation to God. So two things have to be done, one with regard to the neighbor who has been disadvantaged and another with regard to God.

Israelite law is very down-to-earth and business-like. It dictates first of all that the guilty person must return any dishonestly gained property to the one from whom it was taken, to the last penny. To this, twenty percent must be added as grief money. Who knows how much the injured party has suffered as a result of the robbery? And the guilty person must also make the matter right with the Lord—hence the "ram of atonement" (v. 8) that the priest must offer on the altar on behalf of the delinquent. Only when both reparations have been made will the guilty person's relationship with both fellow human beings and God be restored. Verse 7 immediately adds something striking, however: before restitution is made or the ram is offered, the sin has to be confessed. Sincere acknowledgment of sin is the beginning of restoration.

Verse 8 deals with the case in which the injured party is no longer alive and in which his next of kin, the so-called redeemer, has assumed his rights and duties. This survivor is obviously entitled to receive the restitution, just as he would be obligated to help an impoverished next of kin. If there is no redeemer, the guilty party is directed to pay the money back to the Lord—which in practice means that it would go to the priest.

Verses 9 and 10 really have nothing to do with the preceding section. From the subject of compensation—a compensation that in some cases accrues to the priest—the text passes on to the subject of priestly rights. It is hard to translate verse 10, but the most responsible translation would read something like this: "and when someone (brings) his sacred gifts, they will be his: and when someone gives (something) to the priest, it will be his." This means that the sacred gifts that all Israelites offered to the Lord remained their property after they were offered. They had the option of either giving them to the priest as a contribution or designating them for a different purpose. If they chose to give something to the priest, the gift then became the possession of the cult servant.

THE SUSPICION OF INFIDELITY 5:11-31

The difficulties that confront us in verses 13 and 14 can best be resolved if we understand them to present two separate cases rather than a single case. Verse 13 presents the situation of a woman who has in fact gone astray. A man other than her husband has slept with her, but it cannot be proved. Her husband has not seen it; she did it in secret; there were no witnesses, and she was not caught in the act. The prescribed measures that follow are intended to prove her guilt and thus to provide the deceived spouse some legal protection. Verse 14 presents the situation of a woman who may be either guilty or innocent, but who in one way or another has aroused suspicion in her husband. This suspicion grows till he is carried away by a spirit of jealousy. He is convinced he is right and wants to have it established so that he can punish her for her misdeed. The prescribed measures that follow are intended to establish what has really happened and thus to ensure legal protection to the spouse if she has been falsely accused.

Now, what measures are to be taken? In neither the first nor the second case is there proof of the sin, and a trial without evidence would be sure to fail. The alternative offered here is an appeal to the priest—which constitutes, ultimately, an appeal to the Lord. The religious dimension comes to expression in various ways. The husband would bring his accused wife to the priest. The priest in turn would have her stand before the Lord. Her hair would be loosened so that she looked like a woman in mourning. The cereal offering was a reminder offering, meant to call the sins into remembrance. She would have to testify to her total agreement and consent by twice saying "Amen."

We know of measures prescribed in Babylonian law for similar situations. If a husband accused his wife of adultery but she was not caught in the act, then the woman would be asked to declare under oath that she was innocent; if she did so, she would be freed. If a woman were accused of adultery by someone other than her husband, she would be compelled to undergo an "ordeal by water"—to throw herself into the river; if she survived the ordeal, it was taken to be a sign of her innocence. In Numbers 5:11-31 we encounter both prescriptions—the oath as well as the water ordeal (though in different forms). It is possible that the reminder offering was also meant to serve as a test to get at the facts.

With a view to the ordeal, the husband would bring a cereal offering of approximately two quarts to be offered to the Lord on behalf of the woman. In light of the fact that the woman might be innocent, the offering was to be comparatively modest: it was to be composed of ordinary barley flour rather than fine wheat flour, and there was to be no addition of oil or incense (cf. Lev. 5:11b). This offering, which was meant to bring possible transgressions to light, would be placed by the priest on the palms of the woman's hands.

The second item to be made ready was the water of the ordeal. There are different interpretations of what the term "bitter water" here means. Modern English translations (based on the Targum and Vulgate) suggest that it was accursed water; the Samaritan text suggests that it was water that brings things to light; the Septuagint suggests that it was water that convicts one of sin. In any case, the bitter water was composed of three things: holy water, probably water from the large laver; holy dust scooped up from the floor of the sanctuary; and words of cursing, which would be written on a page and then dissolved in the mixture of water and dust. When the woman would swallow this mixture, the curse would enter her totally.

The third element was the curse itself. The priest would clearly posit the two possibilities. If the accused had not committed adultery, her innocence would be signified by the fact that she suffered no ill consequences from drinking the mixture. If she had been unfaithful to her husband, however, the curse-filled water would have a devastating effect. Her thighs would waste away and her abdomen would swell up. This means, at the very least, that she would not be able to bear children.

Having specified the two possibilities, the priest would place the prescribed part of the offering on the altar, and the woman would give her consent and drink the water containing the curse. If proven innocent, she would be able to bear children. If proven guilty, she would suffer the ruinous effect of the curse.

Verses 29 and 30 sum up the two possibilities as follows: either the woman is guilty but it cannot be proved, or it is uncertain whether she is guilty but the husband is possessed by a spirit of jealousy. In either case the husband could make an appeal to the law on jealousy. According to verse 31, he could make this appeal with impunity if his wife proved to be guilty. An adulterous wife could not escape the punishment she deserved, but an innocent wife enjoyed legal protection.

THE NAZIRITE VOW 6:1-8

From the word usage in verse 2, it is obvious that something extraordinary, impressive, marvelous is being referred to in this passage. Someone, either man or woman, makes a vow that for a specific period of time he or she will consecrate himself or herself to the Lord. The Hebrew word has been adopted in English: Nazirite. For the period in which the vow is in force the following three rules apply:

1. The Nazirite must have nothing to do with anything involved in the preparation of wine or any other potentially intoxicating drinks. In itself, wine culture was considered to

be good—Israelites regarded the harvest of their vineyards as a blessing—but there was also a dangerous side to it: the possibility of lapsing into a pagan lifestyle. The time might come, then, when a person would have to refuse to participate.

2. The Nazirite must not cut the hair on his or her head. It must be allowed to grow, even luxuriantly. Perhaps the reason was positive. We know that the warriors mentioned in Judges 5:2, who gave themselves totally for their people, unbound their hair as a sign of their devotion (see the marginal note to the verse in the NEB: "those who had flowing locks"). Those who dedicate themselves to the Lord are called to invest all their energies in the service of the Lord. There might also have been a negative reason this proscription. In many nations at this time, people devoted their hair to their gods. Naturally, an Israelite was not permitted to take part in such pagan practices.

3. The Nazirite must not touch the bodies of parents, brothers, or sisters after they have died. The same demand is made of the high priest (see Lev. 21:11). Death is the last enemy to be abolished by the Lord; between him and death there yawns a chasm—and those who are consecrated to him must keep their distance from the dead.

By pursuing a strict line of conduct in these three areas the Nazirites fulfilled the role of pioneers. Some lived as Nazirites for a specific period of time; others, such as Samson and Samuel, were bound by a vow for life. We get an indication of their importance to the religious life of Israel in the indictment Amos leveled against his contemporaries in 700 B.C.: they silenced the prophets and forced the Nazirites to drink wine (Amos 2:11-12).

THE INTERRUPTION OF THE VOW 6:9-12

This passage deals with a situation in which a Nazirite would suddenly and accidentally come into contact with a dead body. Such contact would void his or her consecration and all that had been done to that point in connection with maintaining the vow. Such individuals would have to start again from the beginning. To purify themselves, they would have to shave their head on the seventh day and bring an offering on the eighth. The offering—two doves or two young pigeons—is the same as that required of poor women who have given birth

(Lev. 12:8), poor lepers (Lev. 14:21-22, 30), and those who have a discharge (Lev. 15:14, 29). One of the doves served as a sin offering to atone for the misstep, and the other dove served as an expression of submission to God. Once this procedure was followed, the head of the offender could be consecrated anew. A lamb then had to be brought as a guilt offering. It is not clear whether the idea behind this was that God had to be recompensed because the desecration had caused something to be withheld from him or whether it was simply a custom to bring a guilt offering at the time of reconsecration.

THE COMPLETION OF THE VOW 6:13-21

When Nazirites had completed the term of their vow and were ready to return to ordinary life, they were required to carry out certain specific actions, one of which was taking a certain number of offerings to the sanctuary. The resemblance between these offerings and the offerings made at the time of the consecration of priests (see Exod. 29, Lev. 8) is striking, though these were less costly. Naturally, it was the priest who prepared the offerings, which were meant to atone for sin, recognize God's majesty, and establish communion with him and one's fellows. At the door of the tent of meeting—the boundary between the sacred and the ordinary—the Nazirite would cut off his or her hair and then burn it on the altar to ensure that it would not be misused. Some of the gifts were then presented as a "wave offering"—that is, the priest and the Nazirite would wave the items before the altar to signify that they were offering them to the Lord. The Lord would then give them back to the priest. After the period of his consecration was thus concluded, the Nazirite would be free to drink wine.

Amos mentions Nazirites in one breath with prophets, but Numbers puts them more in the company of priests. Verse 21 again refers to the rules for being a Nazirite and stresses that those who had promised more than was required would nonetheless be held to their vows.

THE PRIESTLY BENEDICTION 6:22-27

The benediction the priests were required to pronounce is artfully constructed in the Hebrew:

Line 1: 15 letters, 3 words
Line 2: 20 letters, 5 words
Line 3: 25 letters, 7 words

The blessing is constructed in the singular. It has the form of a cultic determination, a promise, a wish, or a prayer. It expands its ideas through its repetitions, the second part of each line clarifying the first part. The content is as follows: (1) the blessing evidenced is preservation in one's daily life; (2) the making of God's face to shine brings his complete favor into effect; and (3) the lifting up of God's face over his people totally permeates their existence with peace.

The fact that the priestly benediction places God's name before the Israelites indicates that the blessings they enjoy are attributable not to some chain of natural events or to the operation of a magical word, but that it is the Lord who blesses and he alone.

We get an idea of how later Judaism interpreted the priestly benediction from the Targum Pseudo-Jonathan (targums are Aramaic translations/paraphrases of Old Testament Hebrew texts compiled from oral traditions; the Targum Pseudo-Jonathan covers the entire Pentateuch with the exception of a few verses):

> The Lord bless thee in all thy business, and keep thee from demons of the night, and things that cause terror, and from demons of the noon and of the morning, and from malignant spirits and phantoms.
>
> The Lord make His face to shine upon thee, when occupied in the law, and reveal to thee its secrets, and be merciful unto thee.
>
> The Lord lift up his countenance upon thee in thy prayer, and grant thee peace in thy end.

GIFTS AT THE CONSECRATION 7:1-9

Verse 1 tells us that certain decisive actions undertaken by Moses had come to an end. The leaders mentioned in verse 2 "offered and brought" the offerings mentioned in verse 3. The Lord commanded Moses to accept these gifts so that he could turn them over to the clans of the Levites, who were charged with transporting the tent of meeting and all the things pertaining to it (see 3:21-38; 4:15-33). Moses stated that the Merarites, who had to transport the heaviest parts, were to receive four wagons and eight oxen. The Gershonites, who were in charge of the lighter material, were to receive two wagons and four oxen. The Kohathites did not need wagons or animals, because they had already been charged to carry the holy objects on their own shoulders. These gifts, which the leaders brought forward in the way people were accustomed to bring their offerings, were given by them on behalf of all the people for the tent and all that went with it.

TWELVE DAYS, TWELVE TRIBES, TWELVE GIFTS 7:10-88

The Hebrew word translated as "offerings for (the) dedication" of the altar in verse 10 also occurs in Egyptian, where it means "gift, offer, offering." In this passage it refers to the dedication of the altar, a centrally important feature of the sanctuary. The gifts of all the different tribes were brought by the leaders mentioned in 1:5-15 but in the order in which they are listed in chapter 2. Regardless of the numerical size of their tribe, they all brought the same gifts. A different leader came each day for twelve days, apparently without making an exception for the seventh day. Thus the emphasis lies on the act of each one personally. The account may strike us as repetitious, but this sort of formula was used by people in the ancient Near Eastern world to reflect ever-increasing joy: look how much these many people gave for the altar!

The kinds of offerings brought cover virtually the entire range of worship in the sanctuary. The largest was the fellowship offering—which indicates that many participants were expected for the sacred meal. Next in size was the offering to God's majesty, an expression of surrender to and reverence before the Lord. After that came the sin offering, an offering we see again and again, inasmuch as sin returns again and again. And finally there is the offering of incense. The homage offering, consisting of fine flour and oil is closely associated with the offering to God's majesty. The total number of animals brought forward was thirty-six oxen, seventy-two rams, seventy-two ram lambs, and seventy-two male goats.

The objects of silver and gold were closely connected with the actions to be accomplished on or near the altar. It appears that ten shekels equaled about four ounces. This would mean that altogether the tribes brought three pounds of gold and sixty pounds of silver in these offerings. Verses 2-9 describe the gifts that were needed for the transportation of the tent and everything belonging to it; verses 10-88 describe the altar on which and by which the sacrificial rites took place. The linking of the two sections indicates that full attention was paid to both the tent and the altar.

THE LORD SPEAKS 7:89

What was given as a promise in Exodus 25:22 literally comes to fulfillment in this remarkable conclusion of chapter 7. The exceptional standing of Moses is evident in the fact that he was permitted to enter the sanctuary on his own to speak with the Lord. Every time he did so he heard the voice. The Hebrew text characteristically omits the name of the Lord in describing the voice, but the Septuagint makes it clear: it was the Lord's voice that Moses heard. The Septuagint also uses a form of a verb that could be rendered "speaking with oneself," possibly suggesting that the situation was more a case of Moses over-hearing the Lord talking to himself than it was of the Lord directly addressing him—a situation like that in 1 Kings 22:19-23, where we read that the prophet Michaiah, son of Imlah, overheard the counsels of heaven. In any case, Moses heard the words of the Lord. The voice emanated from the atonement cover—the mercy seat—lying on top of the ark. The edges of this cover were shaped in such a fashion that, with the addition of the cherubim (sculptures of winged beings), the whole had the appearance of a throne. From this seat the king of kings spoke to his trusted servant.

THE LAMPSTAND 8:1-4

Exodus 25:31-40 and 37:17-24 provide elaborate descriptions of the golden lampstand, mentioning decorative features in the shape of flower-like cups, buds, and blossoms. The description in verses 1-4 here is restricted to just two matters. First, the lampstand had to be made of one piece of solid gold, ham-mered out in a downward direction to a heavy base and in an upward direction to flower-like ornamental work befitting its status as a true piece of art. Second, the oil cups were appar-ently loose. It was Aaron's task to position the cups so that the light of all seven would fall forward, in the direction of the table of the showbread.

THE CONSECRATION OF THE LEVITES AND THEIR TERM OF SERVICE 8:5-26

This passage outlines the procedures by which the Levites were consecrated for their tasks. There are some repetitions, but they do not make for complete clarity. For example, we are not always sure of the order in which the actions were to take place or who it was that performed the rite of the wave offering. Nevertheless, the passage does make several points clear.

The central concept is spelled out in verse 14: the Levites were to be set apart. Out of all the nations, the Lord had set apart Israel; out of all the Israelites, he had set apart the Levites; out of all the Levites, he had set apart the priests; out of all the priests, he had set apart the high priest. And he appointed Moses to set apart the Levites from the rest of the people.

The first action was to sprinkle the water of purification on them. After that, the Levites themselves became active by shaving their bodies (or having them shaven), by washing their clothes, and by purifying themselves. According to a remark made by the Greek historian Herodotus (fifth century B.C.), the priests of Egypt engaged in similar actions, shaving themselves and washing their clothes: "The priests shave their bodies every three days so that neither lice or any other dirt will come in between when they minister to the gods," and "they always wear freshly washed linen clothing." As a result of the water of purification, the removal of all their hair, and the clean clothes, the Levites became, as it were, new people.

Next, Moses brought the Levites and the people together at the front of the tent. He brought the Levites before the Lord, and then the people laid their hands on them as was done with sacrificial animals. In this manner Israel symbolically offered them to the Lord as its own offering.

After that the people participated in a wave offering before the Lord. We do not know how. Perhaps it all took place in the symbolism of approaching and retreating from the altar; perhaps they proceeded up and down the steps of the great altar. There is also some uncertainty about who it was that led this rite. Verses 11 and 21 indicate that it was Aaron, but verses 13 and 15 suggest it was Moses.

The Levites also offered two bulls as a sacrifice, one as a sin offering and the other as an offering to God's majesty (v. 12). In verse 8 the word for the offering to God's majesty obviously dropped out. By laying their hands on the heads of the animals, the Levites signified that this was their sacrifice and that they were transferring their role to these animals. As such they were reconciled people who had dedicated themselves to God.

From this moment on they were totally taken up in the service of the Lord and given as helpers to the priests. Their "military" service consisted in work done by, to, and in the tent. They were permitted to enter it in order to begin their work.

Verses 16-19 repeat what is said in 3:11-13 about God's claim on the Levites: all the first-born are his, but he accepts the Levites in their place, and then he passes on to the priests. It is the duty of the priests to do what ordinary Israelites really should do—help in the ministry of reconciliation and be on guard to protect the people from disaster.

Verses 20-22 repeat only a few of the actions involved in the process of consecration. It is possible that this passage came from another, much shorter tradition.

Verses 23-26 indicate that the term of service for the Levites was from age 25 to 50. Chapter 4 indicates that term ran from age 30 to 50. Are these two different traditions, going back to different periods in history? Verse 25 states that a Levite could no longer serve in office after age 50, though verse 26 suggests that they could still provide some services, exclusive of any really heavy labor. The Septuagint omits any reference to the possibility of continued service after 50, indicating that it was then time for the younger brothers to take over.

THE BELATED PASSOVER 9:1-14

The numbering of the people referred to in chapter 1 took place on the first day of the second month in the second year after the exodus from Egypt. The events referred to in the first part of chapter 9 took place earlier, in the first month of the same year, thus indicating that chronological order was not decisive in the composition of Numbers.

Chapter 9:1-14 states briefly and succinctly the rules that

apply to the celebration of the Passover: it had to be kept on a fixed day, the fourteenth of Nisan; it had to be celebrated between the two evenings—most likely a reference to twilight; the people had to be in a state of ceremonial cleanness; the sacrificial lamb had to be eaten with unleavened bread and bitter herbs; no bone of the lamb could be broken; and nothing could be left till the following day.

This passage presents a problem that some of the people faced. Some individuals who sincerely wanted to celebrate the Passover were not permitted to do so because they were ceremonially unclean as a result of having touched a corpse. They regarded it as most unfair that they were to be excluded from the Passover, which they believed all Israelites were entitled to celebrate.

Something similar is reported in Numbers 27:1-11 and 36:1-12. In all such cases the people would present the issue to Moses, because they regarded him as the one who would know the right answer. He himself did not know what to say, however, and so he took advantage of his authority to enter the tent of meeting to put the question to the Lord. After a period of time, he was in a position to bring the divine verdict back to the questioners. The Lord's pronouncements in such special cases were accorded general validity and used as precedents for making decisions in related cases.

In providing an answer to the case of an individual rendered unclean by contact with a dead body, the Lord also mentioned the case of those who might have been prevented from celebrating as a result of having been away on a journey at the time of Passover. The Targum Pseudo-Jonathan includes yet more circumstances that would have barred people from the celebration—"leprosy," a discharge, and nocturnal emission. The response concerning all of these situations is that they constitute legitimate reasons for barring the individuals from the celebration of Passover but that such people should be allowed to participate in a celebration exactly one month later, provided they have kept the rules.

The pronouncement also contained the warning that any people who had failed to celebrate the Passover at the appointed time without having any legitimate reason for doing so, any people who refused to bring the offering to which the Lord was entitled and who deliberately refused to commemorate the liberation that the Lord gave to his people—such people would be guilty before the Lord and would have to bear the consequences: exclusion from the community of God's people.

The pronouncement also made allowances for the admission to the celebration of Passover of some people who did not belong to Israel—the "stranger [who] sojourns among you." These people who lived among the Israelites were accorded certain rights and obligations short of full citizenship—considerably more rights and privileges than were accorded to total foreigners. Verse 15 speaks of the sojourner and the native. There are various opinions concerning precisely who the "natives" were. Most scholars believe they were Israelites born in Canaan. Others suggest that they may have been the inhabitants of a land in which neither the Israelites nor the "strangers" among them were natives. If the former is correct, the verse would be saying that the feast was open to Israelites and strangers. If the latter is correct, the verse would be saying that the feast was open to Israelites, strangers, and Canaanites. That would be setting the limits really wide!

Some aspects of this passage are difficult to understand in the context of the period in the wilderness. It seems more likely that the reference is to a later period when the people lived in Canaan, or perhaps even to a period following the captivity.

THE LORD LEADS 9:15-23

The cloud was the visible sign of God's presence. During the day it looked like a column; at night it was as bright as fire. The lifting of the cloud was the sign for the people to break camp and to set out; the descent of the cloud was a sign for the people to encamp. The time of breaking up and setting down was determined by the Lord, as were the duration of the stay of the camp and the direction in which the people were to set out. Unfortunately, the Hebrew text is not always entirely clear on matters of time. For instance, in some contexts the word "days" can mean "a year." Drawing on the ancient translations in Greek, Aramaic, and Latin, I believe we can correctly understand the phrase "a longer time" in verse 22 to mean a year. Thus, it would appear that the people would sometimes break camp after only one night, but at other times would remain in the same place for as long as a year. When they remained in one location for a longer period of time it was possible for them to put the entire system of worship into effect. In any event, everything in the passage indicates that God alone had the leadership. Moses was merely an instrument. And the people were called to live out of the obedience of faith.

THE SILVER TRUMPETS 10:1-10

According to Numbers 9:15-23, the cloud provided the signal for departure; this passage indicates that two trumpets also played an important role. Verses 1-7 relate to the wilderness period. Moses was directed to fashion two silver trumpets, works of art. These were to be used for convening the leaders and the people and also to signal the time of departure to the camps. Verses 8-10 speak of circumstances following the entry into Canaan, when war threatened and when festivals were celebrated. On both occasions the trumpets were needed.

We have gotten some ideas of what they might have looked like from two trumpets that were found in the grave of Pharaoh Tutankhamen (one silver and one brass), from a description given by the Jewish historian Flavius Josephus, and from a relief on the Arch of Titus.

They were used for giving certain signals. The Hebrew has two words for this purpose. According to the Vulgate and the Jewish tradition, the one refers to a drawn-out, uninterrupted sound. We translate it as "to blow." The other refers to short interrupted notes (three of them, according to later Judaism). We translate it as "to sound an alarm."

The blowing of the trumpet took place when the people or their leaders had to assemble at the tent. In later ages this sound was made in connection with special memorial days in the sanctuary. When they heard the trumpet sound an alarm, the people understood it as a signal to set out again in the wilderness. The Hebrew text mentions only the divisions encamped on the east and on the south side. The Samaritan text mentions the eastern and the northern group. Only the Septuagint mentions all four. In later ages in Canaan, when the trumpet sounded the alarm, it was a signal that the people were to wage war.

According to verse 8, the trumpets had to be blown by the priests—yet another indication of the centrality of service to

God in the life of Israel. It was the priests who indicated when people had to come together in the tent or the temple; it was the priests who summoned the people to resume the dangerous journey through the wilderness; it was the priests who called the people to prepare themselves for battle against oppressors.

At the same time, the blowing of the trumpets and the sounding of alarm had to do directly with God. Twice we read that the blowing of the trumpets constituted an appeal to him to graciously remember his people—both in time of peace and in time of war (vv. 9, 10). The short concluding sentence "I am the Lord your God" means "You can rely on me."

THE DEPARTURE FROM SINAI 10:11-28

The order for the numbering was given on the first day of the second month, and the order to break camp was given on the twentieth. The Lord signaled this order by means of the cloud. The cloud lifted up over the tent of meeting, here called the tabernacle of the testimony, passed through the wilderness, and came to rest in the wilderness of Paran. This indicates that the people had to journey in a northerly direction—toward the promised land. In breaking camp and moving on, the people followed the order described in chapter 2. We might also note that the names of the leaders of the various tribes are the same as those mentioned earlier—with one slight difference: the text takes account of the existence of the three groups of Levi's descendants. First to break up and leave after the Judah group and before the Reuben group were the Gershonites and Merarites, whose work it was to carry, respectively, the lighter and the heavier share of the tent and its furnishings. The Kohathites, who had to carry the holy objects on their shoulders, came after the Reuben group and before the Ephraim group. In this way the Gershonites and the Merarites had the time and the opportunity to set up the tent and its furnishings at the new location before the Kohathites would arrive to put the holy objects in place. There was a fixed order in accordance with the Lord's instruction: the cloud gave the signal under the leadership of Moses, and a new lap in the journey had begun.

HOBAB AS GUIDE? 10:29-32

Moses was certain of one thing: the Lord had given a firm promise to Israel, a promise of something good, and he was at work to bring it to fulfillment. At some time in the future the people would get possession of the promised land.

Now, all at once, in verse 29, we are introduced to a person by the name of Hobab. If the text is saying that Reuel was the father-in-law of Moses, then Reuel's son Hobab would have been Moses' brother-in-law. Moses asked this Midianite to accompany Israel to the land of Canaan and promised that if he did so, the people would express their gratitude by letting him share in their future good fortune. But Hobab refused, saying that he preferred to return to his own country. It would appear, then, that the route God's people were taking did not pass through the territory of the Midianites, at least not through the part that Hobab came from. Moses reacted to this negative answer by urging him all the more to join the people. Who better than a nomad knows the right places at which to set up a camp? Hobab could have served Israel as eyes that could observe everything or as an elder who could give wise counsel (as the Septuagint says), or as a leader and guide (as the Vulgate has it). If he would share with the people of God in the crises and cares of the wilderness journey, said Moses, then he would also one day share in the benefits that God would impart. We do not know what his final response was. The text suddenly ends. We do know, however, that one must share in the sufferings and struggles of a people if one is to share in their joys.

THE ARK OF THE LORD 10:33-36

It would seem more appropriate if verse 34 were the last verse of the chapter (as in the Septuagint). Whereas earlier it was the cloud that set the direction for the journey, and in the immediately preceding verses there was mention of Hobab as a possible guide, here in verse 33 it is the ark of the covenant that leads, guiding and accompanying the people from the mountain of the Lord to a place where real rest can be experienced. To that end the ark "exerts itself"—more than a box or a throne, it is said to "set out" and "rest." It is something like a wedding ring: the visible sign of the bond between the Lord and his people.

Indeed, in verses 35-36 it is virtually identical with God himself. Moses addressed the ark as though he were speaking to the Lord. Verse 35 speaks of the horror God could generate among his enemies—a reaction that may remind us of the rugged Psalm 68, especially verse 2. Verse 36 is very different. There we read that God turned in grace toward his people in their overwhelming numbers. It was among them he wanted to dwell; it was them he would lead; it was by his guidance that they would arrive at the place of rest. To the outside world he was the Dreaded One; to his people he was the Compassionate One.

In this context, verse 34 shows us yet another aspect of the role the cloud played: the role of protector. The Septuagint uses a word meaning "to overshadow," and rightly so. The ark pointed the way, but the cloud stretched out over the entire people to protect it from the scorching heat.

TABERAH 11:1-3

The word Taberah means "catching fire" or "burning." In this case it is the fire of the Lord, a word which usually refers to lightning. Whatever the precise nature of this fire, we read that the Lord sent it among the people after they complained to him about "their misfortunes." We do not know why the people kept on complaining, but it is clear that this kind of behavior was not in the least pleasing to the Lord. He expects praise, not self-pity.

His reaction was intense anger, expressed in the fire, which began to rage at the extremities of the camp and threatened to consume everything. Only in the face of punishment did the people relent. They cried out for help to Moses, like defendants who seek out a counselor for help when they know they will have to appear before a judge.

Moses agreed to intercede for the guilty. He placed himself in the breach to reconcile the people with God. The fire did die down, but thereafter the name Taberah served as a potent reminder of both God's judgment and of his compassion.

THE DEMANDS OF THE RABBLE AND THE PEOPLE 11:4-9

The "rabble" referred to in verse 4 was a mixed company of people who came along with the Israelites when they left Egypt. It was among these people that the demands for different, better, and tastier food began. Their strong craving and dissatisfaction evidently spread to the members of the people of God, who themselves picked up the theme and set to wailing in their tents. They were not hungry or thirsty; they were simply weary of the daily manna, despite the fact that this food was a direct gift from God.

Verses 7-9 give some of the details. The manna would come at the same time as the dew. It looked like resinous gum, yellowish and transparent. A similar substance can be found in the Sinai wilderness today—the tamarisk tree produces a very sweet yellow-white secretion, though for only a few weeks beginning in June. The manna, on the other hand, was available in large quantities throughout the year. We read here that it tasted something like cakes made with oil. It could be prepared in a variety of ways so as to taste different.

Nevertheless, there was the cry for meat—and that despite the fact that in ancient times meat was eaten in Israel only on special occasions. In the wilderness it would have been very much a luxury. In any event, the offense of the demand for meat was just part of the larger offense of romanticizing the time in Egypt, where there had always been an abundance of fish and fresh vegetables. They were saying in effect that the entire so-called "deliverance" from slavery had turned out to be one huge disappointment. Their demands for meat and fond reminiscences of the riches in Egypt were at the deepest level an expression of contempt for God's redemption. As verse 20 bluntly puts it, the people had rejected the Lord.

MOSES FIERCELY ACCUSES GOD 11:10-15

Is it any wonder that in response to all this wailing God's anger broke loose—intensely, awesomely, devastatingly? One might expect that in such a situation Moses would have reproved these loud complainers for their demands. But he did not. On the contrary, he leveled a series of reproaches at the Lord— reproaches so severe that we might well marvel that they should have been included in the biblical record, so close do they come to outright blasphemy. Still, there they are. He asked why the care of this whole people should be on his shoulders. The Septuagint uses a word here meaning "onrush, pressure, attack." The Vulgate repeats the "Why?" three times. He proceeded to ask whether the Lord had the right to make him responsible for Israel's whole conduct. Such responsibility, he argued, ought to be placed only on the One who had created the people. Moses reached for an image rarely applied to God—that of a mother. He insisted that he never conceived this child or gave birth to it. No, it was God who brought it into the world and was responsible for it. Drawing on another image—that of the foster mother, wet nurse, or nursemaid, whose duty it was to carry the baby in a fold of her dress against her bosom—he suggested that God was rightly the mother and nursemaid of this people, not he. It was God's responsibility to carry Israel to the promised land, not his.

Pressing further still, Moses complained that he could not handle the responsibility even if God insisted that he do so. No human being could meet the demands of such people. It was too much for him. And so, contending that the whole undertaking was completely hopeless, he stated that it would be better for the Lord to take his life than to leave him in such a plight; he would consider death a special favor under such circumstances. Such a sentiment naturally reminds us of Elijah (1 Kings 19:4) and Jeremiah (15:10; 20:14) and of similar heart-rending words in the book of Job. Indeed, many of God's children thus do battle with their Father when they reach the point at which they can no longer bear their misery.

GOD'S DOUBLE PROMISE 11:16-23

In this passage we read that the Lord answered Moses' bitter complaints by instructing him to select from the whole nation seventy men whom he knew to be leaders and to record their names with a view to bringing them together around the tent of meeting. There the Lord would come down, reveal himself (says the Targum Pseudo-Jonathan), and take a part of the Spirit resting on Moses and confer it on those who had been assembled. Led and equipped by that Spirit, they would then be able to share with Moses the burden of caring for the people.

Then the Lord answered the accusations of the people. He told Moses to summon the people to sanctify themselves in preparation for a solemn religious occasion. A dinner was going to be held that would last not a single day or a few days but a full month. God himself would provide an abundance of meat. But he warned that what would begin as a feast would end as a horror. People would eat so much meat for so long a time that it would come out of their nostrils and they would come to loathe it. The Septuagint refers to cholera, an intestinal disease. The Vulgate speaks of nausea. The Targum Pseudo-Jonathan mentions a stumbling block. The people were to be broken by the experience because they had despised the gift of God, glorified their stay in Egypt, and characterized their redemption from slavery as a meaningless event.

In verses 21-23 we encounter a remarkable discussion. Moses implies that the fulfillment of such a great promise is impossible. To feed so many numerous people with an abundance of meat for an entire month—impossible! How many oxen, sheep, and goats would it not take? And how many fish would the pools, rivers, and seas not have to produce? Such is the question that comes up in age after age in the hearts not only of the great like Moses here and Abraham in Genesis 15:2, but in the hearts of the little ones as well. Promise and fulfillment seem to be mutually exclusive. The Lord responds by asking whether anything is impossible for the Almighty, whether there is anything beyond the reach of his hand. The answer he expects to this question is faith. Fulfillment is considerably closer than Moses suspects, and he is about to see it with his own eyes.

THE FULFILLMENT 11:24-35

Verse 24 refers to verses 16 and 17. Moses stations the elders around the tent. Then the Lord descends in the cloud. He proceeds to fulfill his promise by taking a part of the Spirit that rests on Moses and conferring it on the elders. The result is that they begin to prophesy. The nature of this prophecy is probably like that which prevailed among the groups of prophets in the days of Samuel and Saul. They are totally immersed in song, shouting, and praises. Evidently, such a start is a necessity for people who are called to share the burden of leading the people. The last word of verse 25 can be read either as "continue" (Targum Onkelas, Vulgate) or as "stop" (Septuagint). The ancient versions already had to make a choice. From verse 30 we conclude that they stopped prophesying after that one time.

Verses 26-29 constitute a remarkable interlude. Two men of the men who had been summoned to appear at the tent remained in the camp for a reason not known to us. Nevertheless, the Spirit alit upon them too, and like the others around the tent, they also began to prophesy. Predictably, this caused an uproar. A young man immediately reported it to Moses. Joshua, Moses' servant from his youth (or, as the ancient versions have it, "from the circle of his chosen men"), reacted sharply with a demand that Moses silence the prophesying of these two. Such disorderly ecstasy constituted a violation of Moses' authority, he insisted. Moses' answer may come as a surprise. First, he asked Joshua, "Are you jealous on my account?" (NEB). Behind these words lay a world of faith. We see that Moses understood that the issue was not for him to decide but for God. If necessary God would act on his servant's behalf. We can also see in Moses' words the point that it was not Joshua's calling to fight for Moses but to lead God's people in the future. The second statement Moses made was a prayer or wish that likewise implies a world of faith on his behalf. First the Spirit rested only on Moses. Then it came to rest upon the seventy (some say 68, others 72) who prophesied. Next, the Spirit came over Eldad and Medad, thus manifesting itself outside of the existing order, going beyond its limits. Finally, there would be no limits. All the members of the people would be touched by the Spirit. This final step is again envisioned in Joel 2:28-32, and fulfilled in Acts 2 (note the reference to the passage in Joel in Acts 2:16-21).

Verses 31-35 pick up the thread begun in verses 18-23. In the spring of the year quail migrate from the south to the north, and in the fall of the year they fly back the same way. Their numbers are enormous. Becoming exhausted over the Sinai peninsula, they stop to rest along the way and become an easy prey for desert dwellers. In the period when Israel was encamped near Kibroth-hattaavah, huge swarms of quail came down and could be caught at ground level for miles around. The fact that this event occurred as a result of divine intervention is evident from the words "there went forth a wind from the Lord." He was at work preparing an enormous meal for a querulous people. There is some difference of opinion concerning the meaning of the phrase containing the words "two cubits" (= about one yard) in verse 31. The Vulgate interprets it to mean that the birds flew only about one yard above the ground and so could easily be caught. But, as the RSV suggests, it can also be read as indicating that the ground was covered with a layer of birds a yard deep. Such an understanding is clearly consistent with the idea of an enormously large catch. We read that no one gathered fewer than ten homers (a homer has been variously estimated to equal 3.8 to 6.5 bushels). One can hardly imagine what the largest of the gatherings must have amounted to. Unbelievable! But that is precisely the point of the whole story: an inconceivably large mass of birds!

The people spread the birds out on the ground (v. 32) to dry them in order to to keep them from rotting. The table was ready and the feast could begin. But it turned all at once to horror. The people had hardly sunk their teeth into the meat when they were struck a stupendous blow. We do not know exactly what happened, but we know that a very large number of them fell down dead. There were many (mass?) graves. The name of the place where it happened preserves the memory of this appalling event: Kibroth-hattaavah means "graves of greed." Psalm 78:27-31 recounts the awful story in song. Let the people beware!

MIRIAM AND AARON AGAINST MOSES 12:1-16

According to verse 1, Miriam, with support from Aaron, attacked Moses on the issue of his marriage to a Cushite woman. The ancient translations link the woman with Ethiopia, but it is more likely that she came from the Cushan region near Midian. The accusation probably does not concern Zipporah, for Moses had long been married to her. Was this woman a second wife then? Or had Zipporah died and Moses subsequently remarried this woman from Cushan? We do not know.

In any case, verse 2 explains what is behind the conduct of Miriam and Aaron: they envied Moses because God had appointed him to be prophet and mediary for his people. They act as if the Lord had totally overlooked them, but we know this was not the case. Miriam is referred to as a prophetess in Exodus 15:20, and Aaron was the high priest who could make the will of God known to his people through the casting of lots. At bottom, their complaints are directed against God— hence the remark in verse 2, "And the Lord heard it."

Verse 3 tells us something about Moses, a man who sometimes reacted very intensely. It is said that he was of all men the most meek. The word translated "meek" really describes someone who is somehow caught in a trap and cannot expect help from anyone but God; he trusts God completely and surrenders to him. Such meekness is not so much a character trait as it is a faith posture. It explains why Moses did not defend himself against the complaints.

In verse 4 we read that God entered the scene. As the supreme Judge, he summoned the three to the tent of meeting, the place where God and the people meet. He descended in the cloud, positioned himself at the entrance, and told Aaron and Miriam to step forward. We hear not a word about any kind of defense; there was only a sharp indictment from the side of God. Usually he made himself known to prophets by a vision during the day or by a dream at night. We have many examples of such communications throughout the entire history of Israel. But the case of Moses was very different. Just as Joseph had been faithful in the house of Potiphar (Gen. 39:6), so Moses had been faithful in the house of God (we may consider this a reference to the whole nation). On the basis of this trust there was a personal bond between them that was manifested in the way he spoke with his servant—directly, without aids; clearly, not in riddles. The highest distinction was that he was allowed to see the very form of the Lord. No one could see him and live. A few individuals (see Amos 9:1; Isa. 6:1; Ezek. 1:28) were allowed a glimpse, and how reverently the text mentions these things. Moses, however, was permitted to see the form of God. Apart from the Vulgate, none of the ancient versions dared put it like that. They speak of the glory of God and of the likeness of that glory, and do so with great reverence. In any event, how could Miriam and Aaron presume to speak with such rancor to Moses? How dare they! Therein lay their judgment.

The moment the Lord withdrew, they found that Miriam had been stricken with the dread disease of "leprosy," a true harbinger of death. The image of the half-rotted miscarriage (v. 12) is appropriate. Aaron saw it and cried out to Moses for help. Also on behalf of his sister, Aaron made a complete confession of sin, acknowledging their foolishness in acting as they had. With deep respect he asked that the burden of sin might be taken from them. Only then did Moses open his mouth, not speaking for himself, because the supreme Judge had already done that, but for her who had wrongly suspected him of pride. Only the person who had put his own distress in the hands of God can make a plea on behalf of a guilty opponent. How short and how deep that prayer was!

And it was heard. Miriam was healed. But sin is costly to

believers. She was sentenced to be shut out of the community for a week. She could return to life in the community only after she had borne her disgrace. Verse 14 pictures the depth of that disgrace by comparing it to that of a daughter who has been guilty of such misconduct that her own father spits in her face.

THE SPIES IN CANAAN 13:1-26

It would very much appear that at least two traditions have been combined in chapters 13 and 14: one that deals primarily with the tribe of Judah, which suggests that the spies penetrated the land as far as Hebron, the later capital of the tribe of Judah; and another which suggests that all the tribes were involved, each tribe contributing one spy, which altogether penetrated the country to a point far in the north. It is not possible to separate the two traditions completely, although we are able to say when one or the other comes to the fore.

In 13:2 we read that the Lord gave the command for the mission of the spies, which was a part of his work to fulfill his promise of the promised land. In Deuteronomy 1:20-23 we read that the initiative came from the side of the people and that Moses endorsed it. The two accounts are simply two sides of the same coin. Those who were sent out were all chosen from among the leaders of the tribes, though we do not find any of their names recorded in chapters 1 or 7. Again it is striking to note that here, as in the earlier list, there is not a single name in which the divine name YHWH (the Lord) occurs; the name El (God) does occur, however. The note in verse 16 is significant: Moses changed the name of Hoshea to Joshua, which means "the Lord is redemption." And again, since the tribe of Levi did not send a spy on the overtly military mission, spies were sent from the two halves of the tribe of Joseph—Ephraim and Manasseh—so that the total of twelve remains.

From the wilderness at Paran they proceeded northward into the Negeb and from there into the hill country. Their goal was to determine the nature and the number of the inhabitants of the land, the condition the country was in, how the people lived, and whether the soil was fertile. It took courage and energy to complete this dangerous mission. The spies took off at about the end of July or the beginning of August.

In verse 21 we read that they reached the extreme north. Rehob must have been situated at the beginning of the valley between the Lebanon and the Anti-Lebanon range on the way to Hamath. Verse 22 speaks of a much smaller area, principally Hebron and its vicinity, an area known for its wine culture. From the parenthetical remark we learn that this city was seven years older than Zoan, which we now know as Tanis in the Nile delta. A second note mentions a family of giants that lived in the neighborhood of Hebron whose lineage went back to Anak (v. 28). There are various theories about the meaning of Anak. Some scholars contend it is a name, others that it means "long neck," others that it has something to do with a neck chain, and still others that it is a title referring to a line of rulers. In the Valley of Eshcol the spies cut off a large bunch of grapes, branch and all, and carried it with them between poles to keep it fresh. Together with the other fruits, the grapes constituted visible proof of the fertility of the land. Having returned to Kadesh, at the boundaries of the Paran wilderness and the Zin wilderness, the spies were ready to give their report.

THE REPORT 13:27-33

The report of the spies began well. The land was extremely fertile, they said, and they offered the fruit they had brought back as evidence. But this brief statement of its excellence was dwarfed by a list of insurmountable objections. First of all, the land was not empty but inhabited by a variety of nations— the Amalekites, a nation of nomads who now occupied the steppes and deserts of the Negeb; the Hittites, distant descendants of the once-mighty kingdom of Hatti in Asia Minor; the Hivites mentioned by the Septuagint; the Jebusites, inhabitants of a mighty fortress city called Jerusalem; and the Amorites, a people that spread itself over large areas west of Mesopotamia and produced several kings for the kingdoms of Mesopotamia. The Canaanites, after whom the country was named, lived in the lowlands by the Mediterranean and on both sides of the Jordan. The spies observed that the inhabitants of the land were strong and brave and that they would offer staunch resistance should the Israelites try to invade the country. Later they added that all of them were men of great stature who would be dreadful adversaries to the much smaller men of Israel. To top it all, they spoke of the family of giants named after Anak. Graphically they said that in their own eyes they were grasshoppers by comparison with them, but in the eyes of the giants they were still smaller—no more than gnats.

And then the cities—they seemed impregnable. To the minds of the spies, the cities were exceptionally well-fortified with thick walls and enormous corner towers, and they were situated on elevated lands, which would make them virtually impossible to conquer. Imagine the prospect, for a people that had spent years in the wilderness and steppes and oases, of a city that stood like a fortress, commanding the entire surrounding area.

Finally, the spies spread the rumor that the land, for all its fertility, was treacherous. It devoured its own inhabitants, they said. How? By disasters? Infectious diseases? Wars? We do not know. But everything they said tended to drag the people down in disillusionment and despair. The promise was grand, but the fulfillment was made to appear impossible.

Caleb of the tribe of Judah, the one spy who was convinced that it would be possible to triumph in the land, could not do a thing to stop the slide into hopelessness. He tried to quiet the people down, but his words of encouragement (v. 30) fell on deaf ears.

THE REACTION 14:1-10a

The result of the rebellious speech was appalling. All the people began to shout loudly. After weeping and wailing all through the night, the next day they openly rose up against their leaders. They said they wished they had died in Egypt or, as the next best thing, in the wilderness. What awaited them looked as if it would surpass everything they had gone through in horror. The men would be killed; the women and children would end up in the slave market. That, they complained, was ultimately the evil will of God. He was more a demon than a merciful Father. If things were going to be this bad, the people would be better off going back to Egypt, and to that end they should choose a new leader.

On hearing these dreadful words, Moses and Aaron fell on their faces before all the people. Verse 5 employs three words—"assembly," "congregation," and "people of Israel"—

to bring out the fact that their concern was with all the people and the whole nation in all its aspects.

Then Joshua of the tribe of Ephraim joined Caleb of Judah. Both men tore their clothes as a sign of sorrow and mourning for the attitude of the desperate people. Over against a catalogue of complaints born of unbelief, they set down in a few words what faith means. They stated first of all that the land was very, very good, and second that the Lord was perfectly able to fulfill his promise. But connected with that promise there was, of course, a condition: a sincere and firm confidence. Rebellion against God, a fundamental distrust of his promises, and secret unbelief would doom them.

There was no good reason to be afraid of the nations of Canaan, they said. We can devour them (as the Vulgate renders these words), Caleb and Joshua promised! Their protection has been removed from them, they are vulnerable, whereas we can make the mighty confession "The Lord is with us." Everyone who shared in the conviction expressed in that confession could lay aside all fear.

However, as verse 10a indicates, there was no assent to this courageous witness whatsoever. On the contrary, the people wanted to silence these two forever by stoning them. A grimmer, more negative response is hardly conceivable.

MOSES' PLEA 14:10b-25

In verse 10b we read that the Lord himself intervened. His glory appeared to all of the people, but he no longer addressed them generally. That was finished. The two questions he put to Moses both began with "How long?" As a rule, questions in this form were brought by people to God; here he directed them to man. He had reached a limit. He had done enough marvelous things to arouse Israel to faith and obedience. Now the sickness that killed the Egyptians would wipe out the Israelites: he would unleash a plague. But the ancient promise would remain in effect. The nation as a whole would be barred from entering the land, but a remnant composed of the descendants of Moses—or, as the Samaritan and Septuagint texts have it, of the descendants of the house of his father—would be permitted to enter. That new people would be even larger and stronger than the existing one.

In his plea for the guilty, Moses did not refer to himself

or to the grand promise made to him and his own. He was simply concerned for the preservation of the people as a whole. Verses 13-16 record a passionate speech in which he presented one side of the issue.

He spoke of the Egyptians who knew that the liberation of the Israelites was accomplished by the power of God and who related it to the inhabitants of Canaan. Both nations knew what the Lord had done for Israel during the journey in the wilderness. It had been clearly demonstrated that he was with his people day and night. If he now wiped out all of Israel in one stroke, the nations would say he had done so because he was not able to bring his people into Canaan. He was able to liberate them from Egypt and lead them through the wilderness, but for the entry into Canaan his resources fell short. So, said Moses, God's name was at stake—his omnipotence. In the Septuagint, which has a clearer text, we find the same argument.

As verses 17-19 indicate, Moses went on to present another side of the issue: God's patience, his covenant faithfulness, his readiness to forgive the sins of his people—such is his power. At the same time, there is his retributive justice, which does not leave sin unpunished but allows it to work itself out in its consequences for two, three, or four generations. That, too, is within his power. Having confessed his power both to forgive and to punish, Moses made an appeal to the former. Not only is this capacity to be gracious very real, he said, but it is also very great and it had been demonstrated to the people over and over since the time of the exodus. Could it be exercised once more? Lord, do forgive! God's power need not be doubted, but was it possible even now, in the tension between mercy and judgment, for the scales to dip to the side of forgiveness?

Verse 20 reports the miracle of forgiveness. There was a "but," however: the people as a whole would not be wiped out, but neither would the transgressors enter the promised land. The Lord declared under oath that not one of the people who had experienced his power and mercy and then responded with rebellion again and again and had put him to the test ten times (a round number) would enter Canaan. Only the small children who did not yet have any consciousness of good and evil, says the text of the Septuagint, would personally see the fulfillment of the promise. Of the adults then living, only Caleb would be spared, for he alone remained faithful and openly expressed his faith. And indeed it was the descendants of Caleb who later came to possess Hebron (see Josh. 14:13; 15:13; Judg. 1:20). The fact that Joshua is not mentioned in verse 24 suggests that this passage comes to us from the Judah tradition. Verse 30 tell us the Ephraimite Joshua also entered the promised land.

The orders for the next day were to turn around and go back into the wilderness. The journey that had taken them from the Red Sea to Canaan was now being reversed. The forty days of spying was not followed by the conquest of the land. That was now left to the next generation. The reference to the Amalekites and the Canaanites in verse 25 may be an indication that the road to the north was, and remained, blocked.

A PARALLEL REPORT 14:26-38

Verses 26-38 largely repeat what was said in verses 1-25; only the slant is somewhat different. The passage also presupposes that the whole land had been spied out, inasmuch as Joshua is mentioned along with Caleb. The core of the passage consists in the continual repetition of the words concerning the rebelliousness of the spies and of the people. When the Lord asked "How long?" he meant this was the end. The oath formula "As I live" was the strongest denial conceivable. The things he said next were irrevocably going to happen. That is what lies behind verses 28, 30, and 35.

In so speaking the Lord held the rebels to their own words. They had said they would not enter the land, and so they would not. They had talked about dying in the wilderness, and so they would. They had spoken of God's evil intentions, and so they would be struck down by him. But it was all their own fault. We read in the original Hebrew of verse 30 that the Lord had earlier lifted up his hand (a gesture signifying that one is swearing an oath) to give them the land and was now swearing a new oath that he was certainly not going to give them the land—but the change was due not to him but to those who in their rebelliousness had hindered the fulfillment of the promise.

Had the promise, made under oath, been totally canceled out then? In no way. Verses 30 and 38 indicate that Joshua and Caleb would enter the promised land, and of course all the little children who did not yet have a knowledge of good and evil would not be held responsible for what happened and therefore would not be punished. The rebels said, "the children will become "spoils of war'" (v. 31, NEB); God said, "they will enter the land." The rebels spoke of an evil land; their children would discover how good it was. The older generation was brimful of distrust; would the new generation consist of believers? The line of demarcation was faith versus unbelief. The ten spies who by their evil reporting caused the people to rebel were punished by death on the spot, struck down by a divine visitation of the plague (vv. 36-37). The rest of that entire generation—apart from Caleb and Joshua—was condemned to die in the desert sooner or later. The round number forty (v. 34) may refer to a human lifetime: generally speaking, everyone above the age of twenty would die in the wilderness in a period of forty years, because very few people lived beyond the age of sixty. There is a curious connection between the forty days of preparation for an entry that did not take place and forty years of awesome preparation for an entry that would take place—but only for a new generation. In this fashion the people would be faced with the significance of their resistance as well as the wrath, the vengeance, and the retribution of the Lord.

OBEDIENCE THAT CAME TOO LATE 14:39-45

After Moses brought the dreadful message to the people, they plunged into mourning. The next morning they got up early in order, still, to obey the earlier command of the Lord to invade the land from the south, admitting meanwhile that they had been wrong.

They were too late. God's new command was that they should turn around, go back into the wilderness. When they refused to do this, Moses asked them why they were opposing the Lord's command anew. The undertaking would not succeed. Without God's help they would be destroyed by the Amalekites, nomads trained for battle in the wilderness, and the Canaanites, skilled in a war fought in valleys, with fortified cities to fall back on. Their venture was doomed not because their foes were militarily stronger than they but because of a more important weakness in themselves: they had turned their backs on the Lord, and he would now turn his back on them.

Essentially Moses was saying here what Joshua and Caleb had already said: with God, the strongest enemies can be defeated; without him, the weakest opponents can destroy Israel.

Despite the warning, the people still went after their enemies. But the ark of the Lord remained in the camp, and Moses did not go out with them. They went out very much themselves, without God. Is it any wonder that before they had reached the heights of the hill country they suffered a devastating defeat and were scattered by Amalekites and Canaanites? The name of the place of disaster forever bears the memory of it: Hormah, meaning "ban," "destruction."

REGULATIONS CONCERNING CERTAIN OFFERINGS
15:1-16

The regulations outlined in this passage clearly applied to Israel's life in the promised land. The offerings involve the fruits of agriculture—fine flour, olive oil, and particularly wine—in addition to animal sacrifices and thus imply a settled life. They are prescribed for three specific occasions: the fulfillment of a special vow, the spontaneous expression of thanks for benefits received from the Lord, and special days and high festivals.

The animals specified—a young bull, a full-grown ram, and a male lamb a year old—are special sacrifices meant for God. The ultimate goal is to achieve a state of rest between him and his people. When these animals were sacrificed, it was necessary to append specific homage offerings and drink offerings in the following proportions:

	Male Lamb	Ram	Young Bull
Fine flour	1	2	3
Oil	3	4	6
Wine	3	4	6

This means that the more valuable the animal was, the more costly the added gifts. The order of increase is not entirely regular; if it had been, the call would not have been for one-fourth a hin of oil and one-fourth a hin of wine but one-sixth a hin of each.

The term "pleasing odor" (v. 3) has been reproduced in

the Septuagint as "sweet-smelling odor" and in the targums as "a gift which the Lord accepts with pleasure."

These directions indicate how every offering was to be constituted; when there were several, each one had to be in accordance with the same rule. Every Israelite was obligated to comply with these rules. Moreover, verses 14-16 indicate that the regulations extended even beyond the circle of Israel. Foreigners and those resident aliens who had for generations lived among the Israelites were included (at least we may assume that it was these people who were being referred to in the phrase "any one . . . among you throughout your generations" in v. 14). So the window that opens on the nations was becoming wider.

The same prescribed ritual applied to all in pursuing the one goal: God's gracious good pleasure.

A LEVY FOR THE LORD 15:17-21

Throughout the Old Testament we find reminders that the harvest is a gift from Israel's God. Leviticus 23:10 requires the people to bring the first sheaf of unthreshed grain as a thank offering to the sanctuary. Numbers 18:12 calls for the firstfruits of the grain that has been threshed, while Numbers 15:20-21 calls for some kind of preparation of the flour made from the grain—dough, paste, or cake. Commentators generally assume that the references are to barley, barley meal, or barley dough. In any case, it was something that could be used to make cakes. The intent was to stress the point generation after generation that food, even in small quantities, comes from the Lord. In later Judaism the part to be given to the Lord as his levy was set at one-twenty-fourth for one who did his own baking and at one-forty-eighth for bakers.

SIN BY INADVERTENCE AND SIN BY INTENTION 15:22-31

As verse 26 indicates, the responsibility for the error being discussed in verses 22-26 lay upon the people as a whole. They had unintentionally failed to keep one or more of the Lord's commands. Verse 24 does not say how the unintentional sin came to light, but it does imply it had. It concerned commands that the Lord had clearly revealed through the ministry of

Moses and that had been passed down from generation to generation—which suggests that the passage presupposes a long history following the journey through the wilderness. At this point, immediately after the error had come to light, it was time to take measures to remove the guilt. If this were not done, a burden would continue to rest on the people, and in the end they would succumb to it. The offerings required as an atonement for the transgression of the entire nation were a young bull as an offering to God's majesty (along with the appropriate homage and drink offerings) and a male goat as a sin offering.

Atonement was accomplished through the mediation of the priest, but forgiveness was not his work—that remains God's gift of grace. Verses 25b and 26 say the same thing more briefly and somewhat differently, adding that the resident alien would share in the forgiveness.

Verses 27 and 28 prescribe a female kid as the offering for an individual who has sinned unwittingly. Naturally, the sacrifice for the individual is much smaller than that for the whole community. The phrase "sins unwittingly" is used twice and the phrase "commits an error" once to underscore the fact that the nature of the sin is decisive here: only one guilty of unwitting sin may expect forgiveness after making the prescribed sacrifice. Verse 29 extends the rule to the resident alien.

Verses 30-31, on the other hand, concern those who have sinned consciously and deliberately, with their fists raised up against the Lord. Three phrases make this clear: such persons sin defiantly (NIV), despise the word of the Lord, and break his commands. If people affront the Lord in this fashion, it is meaningless to speak of sacrifices, atonement, and forgiveness. Those who are guilty must bear the consequences of their iniquity. They are to be cut off from the community of God's people irrevocably. No forgiveness is possible any more.

The issue discussed in verses 26-29 is discussed at much greater length in Leviticus 4, where it is applied to the high priest and the entire nation, the leader as well as the individual.

WORKING ON THE SABBATH 15:32-36

This passage reports an incident from the wilderness journey. A man was caught in the act of gathering wood on the Sabbath and was brought before Moses, Aaron, and the whole assembly. Since they did not know what punishment was appropriate for him, they kept him in custody, awaiting direction from God (in this respect the story is reminiscent of Num. 9:1-14).

The Lord delivered his verdict using Moses as intermediary: the man was guilty. The punishment, following a formulation from the penal code of ancient Israel, was death. The hallowing of the Sabbath was so important that one's very life was at stake. The sentence had to be carried out by the entire community—outside the camp, which had to be kept clean of blood. And so, in accordance with the instructions given, it was done. Here the rigorous side of the Sabbath came to expression.

TASSELS OF REMEMBRANCE 15:37-41

In this passage the people are instructed to attach tassels to the corners of their clothes with blue cords. We know of a similar custom in the area east of the Mediterranean concerning the clothes of kings, dignitaries, and military officers, though the colors used there were red and blue. Scholars differ as to whether the tassels were meant to serve as signs of distinction or amulets in these other cultures, but their significance in Israel is made clear here: they were to serve as a reminder of the special relationship between the Lord and his people. In later Judaism the blue coloration symbolized the sea, the firmament, and the throne of God.

Verse 41 says three times that the Lord is the God of Israel. As in the Decalogue, the text refers to liberation from Egypt. The tassels, with their blue threads, were to remind the people of both this redemptive event and their calling as a holy nation. They were called to demonstrate this holiness negatively, by turning from their own thoughts, plans, and decisions, from what they by their own lights perceive to be necessary, desirable, or important. This sort of dependence on themselves always ended in their wandering away from the Lord—in their prostituting themselves, to use the strong word the text itself employs (see v. 39, NIV). They were called to demonstrate their holiness positively by directing their thoughts toward him and his commands and by following them sincerely and in all simplicity. The Targum Pseudo-Jonathan rightly says "You must be holy, behold, like the angels who minister before the Lord."

THE REBELLION 16:1-15

Chapters 16-17 speak of at least three different groups that rise up against Moses and Aaron for various reasons. From ancient times, the phrase rendered "became insolent" in 16:1 of the NIV and as "took men" in 16:2 of the RSV has been variously translated "he said," or "he stood apart." In this case, the English translations give a better sense of the intended meaning. Sometimes the different traditions are so intertwined that it is impossible to say with precision who did what and who experienced what.

The first group was that of Korah, a grandson of Kohath and a great-grandson of Levi. As a Levite, he rebelled against the fact that only the descendants of Aaron were allowed to hold the priestly office.

The second group consisted of Dathan, Abiram, and someone named On, who is mentioned only in verse 1. All three were descendants of Jacob's oldest son, Reuben. They could not accept the fact that Moses, a descendant of the younger son Levi, occupied a position of leadership over all the rest, and they accused him of having appointed himself a prince in order to rule over them.

The third group consisted of 250 men belonging to the "elite" in Israel. They are called "leaders of the congregation, chosen from the assembly, well-known men." It is not reported what tribe or tribes they belonged to. We should not be surprised that as men of standing they might have come into conflict with Moses, who was in a sense their political rival, but 16:17 and 35 would seem to indicate that they were also revolting against Aaron: like Korah, they were also offering incense in fire pans (RSV, "censers"), which suggests that they may have felt that since they had been sanctified they should have been eligible to offer up incense.

In verses 2 and 3 we read that the three groups rose up in unison against Moses and Aaron. Each group had its own reasons for revolting, and yet they did not each bring their complaints separately—the Reubenites objecting to Moses' assumption of authority, say, or the Korah group objecting to Aaron's authority. Rather, they began by saying that all the

Israelites were holy and that the Lord was in the midst of all. On this point they were right, of course: every Israelite was called to be holy and the fact that the Lord was pleased to dwell among them was the foundation of their lives. But to deny, on these grounds, that there were different assignments, tasks, and offices was not correct, unless it was the case that Moses and Aaron had put themselves in high positions. But that was not at all the case. It was certainly not true of Moses, a man who had offered every sort of resistance to God's call. In the end, then, the rebellion was essentially an uprising against the Lord himself, who chose these two for their respective offices.

In verses 4-11, we read that Moses first addressed Korah and his group, calling on them to appear before the Lord the following morning with fire pans with fire in them and incense on them. In ancient Israel, lawsuits would be brought in the morning, and in this case the issue was a lawsuit between the Lord and the Korah group. As Moses put it, God would demonstrate whom he had chosen to perform the priestly office. Verse 8 reports that he accused Korah and his group of gross ingratitude. They already occupied a privileged position, being permitted to draw near to God, performing work in and around the sanctuary and acting as substitutes for the people. Must they now also have the priesthood? Again, their argument was not so much with Aaron (he was not that important) as it was with God.

In verses 12-15 we read that Moses reacted to the resistance of the Reubenites, summoning them to appear in order to present their case in an orderly (legal) session before the Lord. They refused his request twice, both times with the same words. More than that, they hurled the grossest insults at him. He had led the people out of a paradisal land dripping with milk and honey, they said, with the villainous intent of letting them die in the murderous wilderness. He bewitched them with visions of a land of beauty in which every Israelite would have his own piece of land and his own vineyard, they said, but his real purpose was merely to feed an insatiable lust for power and to rule over the people like a prince. The phrase "to make (oneself) a prince" in verse 13 is derived from a word that occurs in both the Assyrian-Babylonian and Egyptian languages and indicates a high rank, even the rank of royalty. If all these accusations were based in fact, Moses would indeed have been an unconscionable dictator. Dathan and Abiram added that they would not be hoodwinked or brainwashed.

Is it any wonder that Moses reacted in great wrath? He had come to the limit of his patience. He did what we read the prophet Jeremiah did in Jeremiah 12:3, and what the unknown psalmist of the time of the exile did in Psalm 137:8: he asked God to turn away from them completely, to pay no attention to their offerings, and so to let them die. Over against the accusations of diabolical villainy he asserted his own strict honesty. He had not taken so much as a donkey from them (the Septuagint, changing one letter, reads "anything desirable"), and he had never harmed anyone. This is a strong and proper defense: our faith is manifest in our deeds.

THE TEST WITH THE FIRE PANS 16:16-22

Verses 16-19a pick up where verses 6-7a left off. The Korah group stationed itself with Moses and Aaron at the entrance of the tent. The focus here, as verse 16 suggests, is on Aaron. Noteworthy in verse 17 is the number of the firepans—250 of them. Was this the precise number of the Korah group? It may be more natural to understand this as meaning that the Korah group was joined by the 250 men of high standing in the congregation. Indeed, there may be cause to suppose that the group was larger still. In the Septuagint text, verse 19 indicates that Korah gathered his own following, but the Hebrew text does not have the possessive pronoun and may therefore refer to the entire fellowship of Israel, in which case his following would have been much larger. Whatever the case, however, both parties stood ready with their fire pans, with fire, incense, and all.

Then the supreme Judge himself appeared in the form of the glory of the Lord and revealed himself to the entire community to show whom he had elected to the office of priest. Three things might have happened at this point: the guilty could have taken the innocent with them into destruction, the innocent could have purchased salvation for the guilty as well as themselves, or the guilty and innocent could have received separate judgments. Verse 21 indicates that it was the last option that was realized. Korah and all his cohorts were doomed, whereas Moses and Aaron were called by the Lord to stand apart and so to be saved.

Verse 22 reports that Moses and Aaron did not immediately withdraw from the scene, however. Instead, they fell down on their faces before the Lord in order to plead for the salvation of the many. Was he not the God who bound himself to the existence of his creatures when he created them, they asked. Surely, they pled, it could not be the intent of the highest Judge to let a whole people pay for the sin of one man or one group. What an extraordinary instance of intercession!

THE EXECUTION OF A JUDGMENT 16:23-35

God's answer, reported in verse 24, is in fact a repetition, addressed this time to the entire congregation: let the innocent separate themselves from the guilty. Verse 24b is strange, however. In verse 19 reference is made to the tent of meeting and the Korah group; in verse 24b the reference is not only to the tent of Korah but also to the tents of Dathan and Abiram. The Septuagint is shorter and clearer, indicating that the people were simply to separate themselves from the group around Korah. Verse 25 links up with verses 12-14, in which we read that Dathan and Abiram refused to obey Moses' summons. Having heard God's judgment, Moses and the elders of Israel went to them. At least Dathan and Abiram were consistent in their attitude. They had refused to go to Moses, but now that he came to them, they awaited him at the entrance of their tents together with their entire families. We cannot deny that they had style. They were prepared to stand by their words— even though those words were evil. God's judgment was about to follow, but it was pronounced in a different fashion than it had been in the case of the Korah group. Moses announced that if he had acted from private motives and sought a high position for himself, then they would be innocent and could go without restraint. But if he had honestly responded to the Lord's calling, then they would be guilty and would have to bear the consequences.

If they were innocent, nothing unusual would happen. The members of the rebellious group would die like other people, when their time came. They would simply fall from the ranks of the living without suffering afflictions that were not the lot of all people. If nothing happened, it could be taken as a vindication of their fierce accusations that Moses had acted selfishly.

But if they were guilty, something very special would happen—something comparable to the awesome work of the creation. The earth, like a monster, would open its mouth and devour the guilty men along with their families and possessions. In one instant they would descend into the realm of the dead. If this were to happen, it could be taken as proof that their accusations had been false, that the Lord was on Moses' side. It is significant that the text (v. 30) makes no mention of Moses himself: the issue was not Moses but rather whether the people had despised the Lord.

Immediately after Moses had spoken, the dreadful event took place. The earth opened its mouth, devouring all the people and everything that belonged to them, and then closed up again. Verse 32 would appear to suggest that the Korah group was swallowed up along with Dathan and Abiram rather than meeting a different end, but other passages leave some question as to whether this was in fact the case. The different traditions are all tightly woven together here in such a way as to make the specific chain of events somewhat unclear. In verse 35 we read that the 250 men who sought to offer incense to the Lord were destroyed separately by fire from the Lord. This is reminiscent of Leviticus 10:2, which reports that the sons of Aaron were consumed by fire from the Lord because they had brought "unholy" fire on the altar.

According to verse 34, all of Israel reacted in terror to the execution of the Lord's judgment and broke up in panic at the prospect of suffering the same fate.

THE FIRE PANS AS A WARNING 16:36-40

Verses 39-40 would seem to follow verse 16 in linking Korah and "his company" with the 250 men of standing. This would seem to imply that Korah and his group, along with the 250 men, were killed by the fire from the Lord because they were unqualified to offer incense and that they did not meet their death with Dathan, Abiram, and On when the earth broke open and devoured them alive. Obviously chapter 16 does not reproduce these events with complete clarity, although in the end the essential message is clear: those who despise the Lord will surely be punished.

Following the mention of the "fall" of the 250 men comes the command to Eleazar to collect the copper fire pans and beat them into thin plating for the large altar in the forecourt. God directed that the fire and the ashes remaining in the fire pans had to be scattered far and wide so that it would as a practical matter disappear from the people. The fire pans and the fire had absorbed something of the holiness of the Lord and so had to be handled with care. The pall of sin had to be transformed at the Lord's command into the positive feature of a warning sign. Let the boundary lines be observed! Only the descendants of Aaron were qualified to bring the offering of incense, because the Lord had chosen them.

THE INCENSE THAT EXPIATES 16:41-50

Although it had been clearly established that the rebels were responsible for their own destruction, the people as a whole held Moses and Aaron responsible for their death. They regarded the wrongdoers as victims and viewed the men whom they had wrongly attacked as guilty.

The Lord intervened in this controversy between the community as a whole and its leaders in a fashion we see described again and again: the cloud covered the tent of meeting and the glory of the Lord manifested itself. Entering the tent, the two leaders put their case before him.

His answer in this case was the same as that reported in Numbers 16:26. There the people were called to separate themselves from the rebellious groups so that they would not be swept along into destruction. Here the two leaders were told to separate themselves from the people in order that they might escape general ruin. Being innocent, they would be spared.

Their reaction was very different on this occasion, however. Instead of thinking of themselves, they were deeply moved by the plight of the doomed people. They both fell on their faces before the Lord. The scene is similar to that described in Psalm 106:23, in which we read of Moses standing in the breach to save his people. Then Moses told Aaron to prepare the offering of incense, specifically instructing him to take the fire from the altar. Aaron then hurried into the midst of the assembled people (or, as the Septuagint has it, the center of the camp). The plague had already killed thousands, and so the high priest came to stand between the dead and the living to effect atonement by means of the offering of incense. The Lord graciously accepted the offering, and the plague stopped. But for some 14,700 people it was too late. How enormous the tension when godly people seek to change an angry God's mind so that his grace may gain the upper hand!

THE TWELVE STAFFS 17:1-13

Verse 5 suggests that rebellions against Moses and Aaron had broken out again, specifically with regard to Aaron's priesthood. At bottom this was rebellion against the Lord, who had elected Aaron. It lay on God's heart as a burden that had to be removed, lest the people die (cf. vv. 5, 10).

In order to end these rebellious complaints once and for all, Moses was instructed to ask for a staff from each of the tribal heads (here described as leaders "according to their fathers' houses"). Each staff was to bear the name of the tribe concerned. The staff of Levi's tribe was to have Aaron's name inscribed in it. There was to be a total of twelve staffs (unless Aaron's staff was the thirteenth, as the Vulgate indicates).

What then happened with each staff was to serve as an indication of what was expected from the tribes. God would use the staffs to settle who it was he meant to have charge of the priestly service. Moses put all the staffs down in the tent of meeting immediately in front of the ark of testimony, the box in which the ten commandments, the rules of the covenant, were kept. Thus everything lay in the hands of the Lord.

The fact that the sign was to be delivered in that precise location was connected with the special significance of the tent. As the RSV puts it, God said that this was the place "where I meet with you" (v. 4). The Septuagint, which shifts two letters, renders this phrase as the place "where I make myself known to you." The Vulgate speaks of it as the place where he speaks with Moses. The instructions are to let the staffs lie there and wait to see what the Lord will say by means of them.

The answer the Lord provided puts one in mind of a time-lapse film that shows a plant sprouting, blossoming, and bearing fruit in accelerated fashion. In just a single night Aaron's staff went through this entire process. When Moses entered the tent the next morning it bore almonds. In nature almond trees are the first to bloom, producing splendid white flowers;

they are awake, as it were, when other trees are still asleep—
which accounts for its Hebrew name: the wakeful tree.

All the staffs looked much the same; all of them seemed
quite dead. And yet one sprouted, blossomed, and bore fruit.
The first to witness this was Moses; next were the tribal heads,
and finally all the Israelites. The message was clear: just as
God could make an apparently dead rod miraculously bear
fruit, so he could elect a line of descendants like any other and
enable it to render priestly service fruitfully.

Finally, with an eye to future generations, the Lord instructed Moses to return Aaron's staff to the sanctuary, where
it might remain to serve as a continuing reminder of the place
of the priests in God's arrangement. If the people would continue to respect this arrangement and cease to engage in rebellions against God, they would not have to fear deadly plagues
on that account.

There was much encouragement in this. At the same time,
however, the presence of God had a fearful side, as we see in
verse 13. An enormous dread came over the people. The RSV
translates the three verbs in the Hebrew text as "to perish,"
"to be undone," and "to die." The Aramaic version recounts
fearsome means of destruction from the past: being slaughtered by the sword, being devoured by the earth, and being
destroyed by the plague. What would become of a complaining, recalcitrant and rebellious people without a priesthood
that could act to make atonement for them?

THE TASKS AND INCOMES OF PRIESTS
AND LEVITES 18:1-32

Since verses 1-7 concern the boundary lines between non-le-
vites, levites, and priests, it is no wonder that Aaron rather
than Moses is addressed by the Lord.

The high priest and the priests are responsible for what
happens around, inside, and generally in connection with the
sanctuary. As verse 1 indicates, they would pay the price for
any violations of the rules concerning the sanctuary as well as
for any violations of the rules committed by or against the
priesthood as a whole.

The real work of the priests is described in verses 5 and
7. The altar features prominently in these verses because it was
here that sacrifices of extreme importance for the entire com-

munity were brought. Special attention is also given to the sanctuary itself, which contained all of the furnishings and accessories needed for the service of worship, and especially to actions that were to be performed behind the veil that separated the Holy Place from the Most Holy Place. The task of the High Priest lay behind the veil. The priests performed their service in the room in front of the veil, which contained the table of the showbread, the lampstand, and the altar of incense. They all had different kinds of work to do in the forecourt, the space that was even nearer to the public. Concerning the task of Aaron and his descendants, verse 7 points out that God gave them their priesthood as a gift.

Verses 2-4 and 6 describe the task of the levites. Verses 2 and 4 indicate that they were to join themselves to the priests (scholars link the name of their ancestor Levi with the Hebrew verb "to join"). At bottom they were people given to the Lord from the midst of the nation as a whole and were therefore called "the given ones" (v. 6). But the Lord in turn passed them on to the priests as a gift. Their most important task was the service they provided in connection with the sanctuary. After the tent of meeting was set up, they would guard it to keep out unqualified persons, and they would also render auxiliary service in worship. When the tent was broken up, it was their duty to see to it that everything was done in an orderly fashion. As such they were indispensable helpers of the priesthood. But they were no more than helpers. They were not permitted behind the veil or near the altar. The same rule applied to priests. All such who approached closer were condemned to death. The ultimate intent of this arrangement was that the wrath of God should not come over the people as a whole.

In verses 8-19 we read that the Lord again spoke to Aaron, this time concerning the priestly dues that came from the offerings and sacrifices the people gave to the Lord. Verse 9 dictates that Aaron and his sons were to receive what was left on the altar of the homage offerings after they had been burnt, of the sin offerings that effected atonement, and of the guilt offerings intended to make up for a misdeed. Verse 11 mentions a part of the wave offerings, which were given to the Lord with a certain ritual movement and then returned. According to verse 12, the wave offerings consisted of the best of the oil, the new wine, and the grain. Verse 13 indicates that they included the firstfruits of everything that grew on the land. Verse 14 adds everything that is withdrawn from ordinary use and "devoted" by a ban to the Lord. Finally, verses 15-17 outline rules concerning the first-born of the clean animals—bulls, sheep, and goats. After the blood had been put on the altar, the priests were to receive the meat. Verse 18 specifies that they were to receive the breast and the right thigh of animals sacrificed in wave offerings.

The priests, together with their sons and sometimes their daughters (those still living at home), were permitted to eat all this. The RSV indicates that the gifts were to be eaten "in a most holy place" (v. 10). The NEB indicates simply that they were to be eaten in a manner that "befits most holy gifts." Leviticus 6:16 does tell us that certain offerings were eaten in a holy place, and it is possible that this is the direction in Numbers 18:8-19 as well. But permission was given to eat at least some of the offerings at home, because both boys and girls were allowed to take part in the meal—provided they were ceremonially clean.

The ultimate purpose of all the offerings was to ensure the good pleasure of the Lord; to eat of them was to have a share in this great benefit. For that reason it is comforting to hear in both verse 8 and 19 that it was a perpetual ordinance. For good measure it is even called "a covenant of salt," as in Leviticus 2:13. At a meal in which a covenant between two parties was sealed, people in ancient times occasionally used salt to signify the incorruptible, firm, and lasting quality of the agreement. The levy of the Lord was actually a levy for him, but he passed it on to the priests, so great was his concern for them, rooted in a firmly established covenant.

The reference to the redemption of the first-born involves both human beings and animals. Naturally human first-born could not be sacrificed; they were to be redeemed at the established price of five shekels of silver (about two ounces). The first-born of unclean animals were either put to death or redeemed; one could redeem them either by replacing them with clean (unblemished) animals or by paying money, according to the rules recorded in Leviticus 27:11-12, 27.

In verses 20-24 we read that the Lord also spoke to Aaron. When the people gained possession of the promised land it was to be divided among the tribes. Every tribe was to get an inheritance that would pass from generation to generation.

This share of inherited possession would constitute the basis of the people's existence. Only the tribe of Levi was excluded from the plan of division. Verse 20 says that the priests would have no inherited possession or share of the possession; verses 23-24 say the same thing of the levites. The Lord himself was to be the inheritance and share of the priests (v. 20). He was the basis of their existence. They could count on him to take care of them. The guidelines established in verses 8-19 and again in verses 25-32 attest to this concern. And the same was true for the levites in this respect too. Nonlevitical Israelites who entered and worked in the sanctuary as the levites did would have been punished with death, but God protected the levites. And as a reward for assuming the task of ensuring the proper course of the liturgy and bearing the iniquity of the people as their representatives (v. 23), they were assured that they would receive tithes of the grain of the land, fruit from the trees, and the increase of herds and flocks (Lev. 27:30-33), or, as Deuteronomy 14:22-23 has it, tithes of the products of the soil, grain, new wine, and oil. Numbers 18:21-24 suggests that the tithes were a levy from the people that they contributed to the Lord and that he provided for the levites by turning the gifts over to them. At the same time, the tithes were considered compensation for their labor in the tent of meeting.

The ordinance concerning the tithes was to apply from generation to generation, thus making the livelihood of the levites secure. The idea behind all this was that the Lord was the owner of the land, and the Israelites had to give to him its best products in the form of firstfruits or a one-tenth share. He would then keep it for himself or give it to his cultic servants or leave it with the owners or in certain cases leave it to the poor by way of the owners.

It is interesting that the Lord addressed Moses concerning the provision that was made for the priests (vv. 25-32). The preceding verses indicate what the levites were to receive, but not the priests. Now we learn that the levites were to regard the tithes they had received as if it were produce they had raised, and they were thus to offer up a tenth of it to the Lord. They were instructed to take this tithe—which had to be the choicest part of what was already the choicest part (literally, the "fat")—and turn it over to Aaron for the priests. Once they had turned over this "devoted" part (devoted to the Lord, and therefore holy—see v. 29), they could with a clear conscience lay claim to what remained and safely eat it anywhere. What they had left was altogether theirs. They could eat of it anywhere, for the "devoted" part had been turned over to them.

For a view of the tithing ordinance as a whole, it is worthwhile to read Nehemiah 10:35-38 alongside this passage.

THE ASHES OF THE RED HEIFER 19:1-10

Could it be that the text of verse 2 originally read not "the statute of the law" but "the statute of the cow," as the Vulgate approximately renders it? Whatever the case, the text speaks of a heifer that must be sacrificed to cleanse those who are unclean.

Several conditions were laid down for the animal that was to be sacrificed. It had to be totally free from blemish or defect, both externally and internally. It had to be completely untouched, "virginal," which is to say that it must never have drawn a plow or a cart and must never have been involved in work on the land. The Targum Pseudo-Jonathan expands the list of rules in keeping with the practices of a later period. The color red was also very important in the ceremony. For one thing, it symbolized blood in a ceremony in which blood itself played an important role (see v. 4). And one of the objects to be thrown into the fire was to be red—namely, the scarlet material mentioned in verse 6. We are not entirely certain what this material might have been. RSV reads "scarlet stuff"; NIV reads "scarlet wool"; NEB reads "scarlet thread." Assuming it to have been wool, we can understand the passage to be saying that just as there can be no forgiveness without the shedding of blood, so there can be no purification without the red color of the hair, the blood, and the wool.

Verse 9 calls the red heifer a sin offering, but the ritual prescribed here is different from that prescribed for sin offerings in Leviticus 4. In this passage no mention is made of making a sacrifice within the sanctuary, of putting blood on the horns of the altar, of pouring out the major part of the blood at the base of the altar, or of burning the fat on the altar. On the contrary, the Lord told Moses and Aaron that the animal was to be immediately brought outside, even outside the camp. There, under the keen supervision of Eleazar, the son of the high priest, it was to be slaughtered and burned entirely—skin, meat, blood, offal, and all—till only the ashes remain. The only rite described here that is associated with sin offerings elsewhere is the direction to take some of the animal's blood on one's finger and sprinkle it in the direction of the Most Holy Place, the place of God's special presence (v. 4).

Verse 6 mentions three more elements that were to be added to the fire in which the heifer was burning: (1) cedar wood, the best and the most expensive wood known, which was also used in purifications in the Babylonian world; (2) hyssop, a small plant that was well-suited for rites of purification (when the plant is dipped in water, its clusters of hairy leaves trap many droplets of the liquid, which can then be sprinkled from the plant onto another surface); and (3) the scarlet material, symbolic of blood. These three, also mentioned in Leviticus 14:4, 6, were all considered to have a purifying effect and were thrown into the midst of burning cadavers. When these ingredients were added to the burning red heifer, the result was considered to have a most extraordinary purifying power.

After everything had turned to ashes, a ceremonially clean man would take the ashes to a ceremonially clean place outside the camp where they would be kept for future use. In later Judaism the ashes were divided in three parts. One part was kept at a designated place in the temple; the second part was kept on the Mount of Olives, where slaughter and burnings had taken place; and the third part was kept in the care of the levites.

It is remarkable that ashes which purified the unclean defiled the clean. The three persons who took part in the rite would all remain unclean till evening and had to bathe themselves with water. The priest was directed to wash his clothes, rinse his body with water, and come into the camp. The man who burned the animal was directed to wash his clothes and bathe his body. The man who gathered up the ashes and put them in storage was directed to wash his clothes. The Targum Pseudo-Jonathan assumes that all three participants in the rite must be priests, but the text makes this requirement only of the one who supervised.

According to verse 10, the rite is to be a perpetual ordinance for the Israelites as well as for the foreigners living among them.

THE APPLICATION 19:11-22

The repetitions in this section are probably due to the combination of different traditions.

There are two circumstances under which a person becomes ceremonially unclean by contact with the sphere of death. The setting of the first is a tent (later, a house). Whoever enters the room where a dead person lies is unclean for seven days. The same applies to all who are in the tent. It may be the case that the text is indicating that things as well as people that enter such rooms, and things that are already in the tent, should also be considered unclean for seven days: verse 15 mentions a container that has not been closed off with a cover and a strong cord and says that its contents should be considered unclean. This is reminiscent of Leviticus 11:32-33.

The setting of the second circumstance in which a person might become ceremonially unclean is the open field, where one might come into contact with someone killed by the sword, with someone who died in solitude, with someone who died a long time before and of whom only the bones are left, or with a grave. The Targum Pseudo-Jonathan is even more detailed on this point, stating that little bones one finds, or parts of the body of someone still living, or parts of a grave such as the stone that closes the opening will all render one unclean by contact.

The text goes on to prescribe the means by which one can be purified of this uncleanness. First, the ashes of the heifer, the cedar wood, the hyssop, and the scarlet material, all of which had been stored away, were to be mixed with fresh spring water, another symbolic means of purification. The resulting mixture was, as it were, a means of purification to the third power. A ceremonially clean man would then have to use a twig of hyssop to sprinkle this mixture on all unclean persons and things, both in the case of a purification done inside a tent and purification done in the field. This rite was to be performed on the third and the seventh day following the defilement. Then, after the unclean person had washed his clothes and bathed his body with water, he could be considered clean on the seventh day. The man who sprinkled the water of impurity would have to wash his clothes. Anyone who touched the water of impurity would be rendered unclean till evening.

This ritual was important not only for those who were

unclean but also for their environment. We can infer this from verse 22, in which we read that everything the unclean person touches becomes unclean and whoever in turn touches the unclean thing also becomes unclean, if only for a short time. Uncleanness, apparently, spreads easily.

Indeed, according to verses 13 and 20, an individual's uncleanness defiled the sanctuary. This is in the spirit of Numbers 5:1-4, which also mentions various forms of defilement: the atmosphere of the God of life is intolerant of the atmosphere of death; between these two a great gulf is fixed.

Those who knowingly persevered in being unclean and refrained from using the means of purification thereby demonstrated that they despised the Lord, who, as the Holy One, desires to live in grace among his people. All who placed themselves outside the community of God's people in this manner were to be cut off from the people (vv. 13, 20).

THE DEATH OF MIRIAM 20:1

Kadesh, also called Kadesh-barnea, was situated close to the place where the wilderness of Paran and the wilderness of Zin came together. The text indicates that the Israelites arrived there in the first month, but it does not say of what year. Was it the year Aaron died, the fortieth since the exodus (33:38)? In any case, it was here that Miriam died. Verses 28-29 describe the death of Aaron. Verse 12 points to the fact that Moses died before the entry into Canaan. None of the three leading figures was allowed to enter the promised land. Verse 1 restricts itself to a sober report concerning the death and burial of Miriam. The Targum Pseudo-Jonathan has more to say on the subject and refers to a well that the people received on the basis of Miriam's merits. When she died, this well was hidden; hence the thirst reported in verse 2. Scholars are not certain where this tale came from.

THE SIN OF MOSES AND AARON 20:2-13

Yet once more the people rebelled against Moses and Aaron. Their indictment is reminiscent of that made by Dathan and Abiram in 16:12-15: they said they wished they had died earlier, at the same time as their fellow citizens who fell in the course of the long journey through the wilderness. The double accusation returns in verses 4 and 5: Why did you take us out of Egypt and into the wilderness in order to die in misery? And why have you made us come up out of Egypt—that is, why did you deceive us with a promise of a land situated on a higher plane? (Canaan does in fact have a higher elevation than the Nile delta.) They complained that Moses and Aaron had conspired to lead all of them, cattle and people, to their deaths in the wilderness. In response to this awful accusation, the two men had only one course open to them: they separated themselves from the many and went to the tent of meeting, where they fell face down before the Lord. Again, verse 6 tells us, the glory of the Lord intervened both to judge and to save.

God's will to save comes out clearly in the words he spoke (vv. 7-8). Moses was to take the staff that lay before the Lord and gather the people to go with him to "the rock"—a reference to a familiar place. What staff is meant here? Was it the one with which Moses had already done so many marvelous signs (Exod. 4:2; 7:15; 9:23; 10:13; 14:16)? The reference to "his" staff (v. 11) might imply this. Or was it Aaron's staff, the one that was laid before the Lord (Num. 17:10)? Arguments can be adduced for both, since both were associated with God's special interventions.

Exodus 17:1-7 tells us that under similar circumstances the Lord had commanded Moses to strike a rock in order to receive water from a subterranean source. This time, however, he received no such command. It was not the staff but only the word, spoken under orders from God, that was to suffice. Moses needed faith of the sort that could move mountains.

The promise was that the moment the word was spoken to the lifeless rock, the miracle would occur before the eyes of all the people and the water would gush from the rock in amounts sufficient to quench the thirst of man and beast. This was God's intention, a change from his attitude in the case of earlier rebellions: here mercy won over judgment. To accept this kindness toward a sinful people demanded even more faith from Moses (especially when we recall Num. 16:15, in which we read that he asked God to turn away from the people who so seriously but falsely accused him). God's power and God's mercy—these are the two focal points that were to be brought once more to the attention of the people.

But at this point both Moses and Aaron failed. Instead of speaking to the rock in faith and trust, Moses spoke in bitterness to the people, calling them rebels (v. 10). Then he asked if the two of them had to bring water out of the rock for the people (the Hebrew idiom allows us to make a choice between "can," "shall" and "must"). In any case, the two men supplanted God as the center of attention. And finally, instead of merely speaking to the rock as he had been told, Moses struck it twice with his rod. The Targum Pseudo-Jonathan shares the curious information that the first time drops of blood appeared, and the second time water gushed out in great quantities. The people got water and a new lease on life, but Moses and Aaron had failed to show them the reflected image of the Holy One, the Wholly Other, the God who is almighty and merciful. For that reason God charged the two with having failed to sanctify him before the people. Moses "spoke words that were rash," says Psalm 106:33 in reference to this incident (Pss. 81:7 and 95:8 also make reference to it). When people fail in so high a calling, they are not permitted to finish their task. God announced that both Aaron and Moses were destined to die in the wilderness.

The name of the place, Meribah (meaning "quarrelling," "contention"), bears a reminder of this extremely sad event.

A PASSAGE THROUGH EDOM? 20:14-21

From Kadesh Moses sent messengers to Edom, which was situated south of the Dead Sea and east of the Israelites' camp. The message he sent was composed in a stereotypical form comprising four parts: an address, an identification of the sender, the reason for writing, and a request. Similar messages have been found recorded on clay tablets in the ruins of the ancient town of Mari on the Euphrates (ca. 1750 B.C.) and in the letters of Revelation 2 and 3 (ca. A.D. 90).

The message incorporates the following information. (1) It is addressed to the king of Edom. (2) The sender is identified as "your brother Israel." (3) The reason for writing includes a description of the misery Israel underwent in Egypt, an appeal to God, an account of his having redeemed the people by means of an angel (a point that underscores the distance between God and man), and finally an acknowledgment that with God's guidance and help they have come to the borders of Edom. And (4) the request is made that Israel, on its way east and north, be allowed to pass through the land of Edom.

Moses promised that the people would keep to the so-called King's Highway (in later ages, "the Sultan's Highway"), along which armies and caravans traveled, and that they would in no way violate the property rights of the Edomites by taking anything from their fields, vineyards, or wells.

Edom's answer was a blunt refusal accompanied by the threat of military action.

There is scholarly debate over whether verse 19 constitutes a second attempt to win consent or reflects a parallel tradition of the same request that is simply worded differently. Again there is mention of a highway (the Septuagint reads "hill country"). The Israelites promised to pay for the water their animals would consume—indicating that they knew some such consumption would be inevitable. They said they only wanted to pass through on foot—nothing extraordinary. But in verse 20 we read that Edom's reaction was even more fierce. They did not restrict themselves to words or threats but came out against Israel with a large and powerful army.

Why didn't Israel fight? Were they afraid they would be overpowered? Perhaps Targum Pseudo-Jonathan is right when it reports that God forbade them to fight because the day of his wrath had not yet come. Perhaps we should bear in mind Deuteronomy 2:5, which says that the Lord gave the hill country of Seir to Edom and not to Israel. It seems quite possible that they would have refrained from battle on account of kinship with the Edomites, descent from a common ancestor. Elsewhere we find that they refrained from declaring war on the Moabites, who were related to Israel by way of Lot, whereas they did not similarly spare the Amorites or the other inhabitants of Canaan. This suggests that the word "brother" in verse 14 had a very real significance. Israel chose another way because the two were, in essence, brothers.

THE DEATH OF AARON 20:22-29

From Kadesh the people took a detour around Edom, marching south in order to be able to go north. There is some scholarly difference of opinion concerning the exact location of Mount Hor. It has traditionally been located near Petra, although that would place it squarely inside Edomite territory. A more likely site, then, is a spot about ten and a half miles south of Kadesh. In any case, it was on Mount Hor that Aaron died. The expression "being gathered to his people" (i.e., ancestors) initially meant being buried in a family grave. Later on it came to have the more general meaning of simply being buried.

The designated successor, after the deaths of Nadab and Abihu, was Eleazar (cf. Lev. 10:12). On orders from the Lord, Moses officiated on top of the mountain at the ceremony transferring the office from father to son. Of the rites prescribed in Leviticus 8 and 9 for this action, only one is clearly mentioned in Numbers 20: the change of high priestly clothing (called, in the Targum Pseudo-Jonathan, the "clothes of the glory of the priesthood"). The first high priest had to make way for his successor, and so the chain continued. People change; the work, in God's name, continues.

Moses carried out his assignment. On top of the mountain there was a changing of the guard. There is a touch of greatness in the quiet ceremony described here. According to Targum Pseudo-Jonathan, Moses came down from the mountain with his clothes torn, and he wept, "Woe is me, on your account, my brother Aaron, pillar of the prayers of Israel." So great was the position of the high priest that instead of the seven days of mourning prescribed for the ordinary Israelite, the mourning for Aaron lasted thirty days, just as it would later for Moses.

HORMAH: BAN (OR DESTRUCTION) 21:1-3

Arad, which modern excavations indicate was about eighteen and a half miles south of Hebron, was an important site in the days of Solomon, being home to a citadel and a shrine. If this is the site being referred to in this passage, then we are here dealing with an area in southern Canaan. Was there a second attempt, thirty-eight years after the first, to penetrate the land from the south? Or did Israel travel in a southeasterly direction around Edom to the east and later to the north, in the process coming under attack from behind by the Canaanite king?

The place called Atharim has not yet been identified. In a number of ancient traditions the word appears as *tarim*, "spies," which would obviously be a reference to the people's sad history. Whatever the case, Israel was defeated here and the enemy took many captives. Under these circumstances, the people made a vow called a "ban" (for a similar vow, see Judg. 11:30-31). Such vows entailed promising to give up all claims

to any booty that might result from victory. Just as in Deuteronomy 7:2 and 20:17 and Joshua 10:28, the text here speaks
only of complete destruction. Other forms of the vow made
allowance for keeping some of the enemy forces alive as spoils
of war. In this case, the Lord responded to the people by utterly
destroying the cities. For Israel, this victory, coming after so
many disappointments, was very encouraging. The name Hormah, "Destruction," came to serve as a reminder of a rescue
given by God.

THE BRONZE SNAKE 21:4-9

The gratitude of the people did not last long. Soon they once
again began to accuse the Lord and Moses of having had evil
intentions in liberating them from Egypt. The whole enterprise
had not brought them to any promised land, they cried; to the
contrary, it had brought them to death in the wilderness. They
had neither bread nor water, they complained, and such food
as they did have (manna, according to the Targum Pseudo-
Jonathan) was horrible. In response the Lord sent snakes among
the people whose deadly poison set the whole body on fire,
as it were. The Septuagint correctly translates the term here as
"killing snakes," although we find a variety of names for them
elsewhere: fiery snakes (RSV, KJV), the serpent (Amos 9:3),
the burning one or seraph (cf. Isa. 6:2); Nehushtan in 2 Kings
18:4 (see the marginal note to this term in the NIV). The poi-
sonous snakes found easy prey among the people. Only when
the death toll began to rise did the people confess they they
had sinned against the Lord and against Moses. They appealed
to Moses to act as a go-between and advocate to avert the
plague. Moses agreed and took up their plea with God.

In answer to Moses' prayer, God ordered that a snake or
"seraph" be made of bronze, placed atop a signaling pole, and
lifted up above the heads of the people. In Mesopotamia the
snake was regarded as a kind of deity. In Egypt the Pharaoh
had a replica of a cobra fixed to his crown for protection.
Archeologists have discovered amulets in the form of snake
figures two and a half to four inches long in Canaan. Such
figures were widely believed to provide a magical means to
avert evil.

The bronze snake spoken of in Numbers 21:4-9 was not
a magical object in any sense, however; rather, it was a sym-

bolic concentration of evil, incarnate sin, the visible sign of human failure. It was lifted high above the people on a standard, a banner, or a sign (as so many ancient translations have it), and as on other occasions reported in the Bible, the people were called to gather around a tall pole. In this case, all who were afflicted with the deadly poison were directed to fix their gaze upon this objectified evil lifted up in the air; those who did so would be healed. The Targum Pseudo-Jonathan adds to the account here, indicating that merely looking at the snake was not enough; it had to be accompanied by a change of heart or it would not be effective. Clearly the command called for both looking up and trusting God's mercy. That is why the incident is referred to in John 3:14: we must not only look to Jesus' being lifted up on the cross but trust in him to receive salvation. When, some five hundred years later, people had come to ascribe magical power to the bronze snake itself (according to 2 Kings 18:4 the Nehushtan had become an object of adoration), the reformer king Hezekiah deemed it necessary to destroy it.

TOWARD THE FIELDS OF MOAB 21:10-20

This passage outlines the route followed by Israel: from Oboth to the Iye-abarim to the Valley of Zered to the Arnon to Beer, Mattanah, Nahaliel, Bamoth, and on to the valley in Moab where the top of Pisgah overlooks the wilderness. Although we are not certain where all of these places were located, we are certain that Israel traversed the entire length of the Dead Sea. The shortest route would have been straight from south to north through Moab, but this would have been difficult for the people since it would have entailed crossing the lower course of the rivers, which were deep. Another route would have taken them around Moab, first traveling east from the south, then going north, and finally going west; although it would have been longer, this path would have presented fewer changes in elevation.

The report of the journey is interrupted a couple of times. Verses 14 and 15 mention some geographic names—Waheb, Suphah, the Arnon river valley, and Ar. The Samaritan text speaks of this region as a gift of God to his people. In the Septuagint the text is distributed differently; it mentions a war of the Lord that set the streams of the Arnon on fire. The

Vulgate, following another reading, says that what happened at the Red Sea was to be repeated at the Arnon. The Targum Pseudo-Jonathan has a long and fantastic story about Edomites and Moabites bent on Israel's destruction who were crushed between mountains that slid together at the Lord's command. In any case, the theme common to all of the translations is that Israel owed its salvation solely to the Lord. The text itself comes from a lost document called "the Book of the Wars of the Lord." It is regrettable that we have available to us only these few damaged lines.

As a marginal note to verse 16 in the RSV indicates, the name Beer means "Well." It was at this spot that God commanded Moses to call the people together in order that he might give water to the thirsty. Verses 17-18 contain a brief poem calling on the well to give water and a song of praise commemorating the fact that it did so. The princes and noblemen used their scepters and staffs to help open up the well. The Targum Pseudo-Jonathan tells a remarkable tale, indicating that this well traveled with the people as they went up into the mountains and down into the valleys. Is it possible that Paul is alluding to this story in 1 Corinthians 10:4?

SIHON OF HESHBON 21:21-32

In this passage we read that the Israelites asked that they be allowed to pass through the land of Sihon the Amorite. The territory in question lay between the Arnon, half way up the Dead Sea, and the Wadi Kefrein to the north of it, with the land of the Amorites to the east of it. The request resembles the one they had made of Edom. Again Israel promised to spare fields, vineyards, and wells and to hold to the King's Highway. But the opening does not follow the lines of a formal message sent by a messenger; there is no mention of the miseries endured in Egypt, and no appeal is made to brotherly sympathy. No wonder, for there was no bond between Israel and the Amorites.

Sihon refused Israel's request point-blank and marched against the people Israel with a large army, intending to wipe them out if possible. The armies met at Jahaz, and Israel so completely defeated the Amorites that they were able to occupy the entire kingdom of Sihon, from the Arnon northward to the Jabbok, north of the Dead Sea. The territory of Jazer, close to the present city of Amman, remained Amorite, forming the border with Ammon. (Verse 24 has been translated in two ways. The Hebrew text has been taken to mean "the boundary was strong"; the Greek text has been taken to mean "the boundary was Jazer." The latter translation is preferable.) Verse 32 also tells us how this piece of Amorite land was conquered: first it was spied out and then it was taken by military action. According to the Hebrew text, Israel conquered all the cities belonging to the territory; according to the Greek text, it conquered Jazer itself. In this way, the people got to see something of the fulfillment of God's promises, although they had not yet reached the real Canaan.

In verses 26-30 we encounter, in poetic form, a piece of the ancient history of this embattled area. It belonged at one time to Moab, but Sihon drove out the Moabites and occupied the conquered territory. Now the Amorite king was in turn being driven out by the Israelites. In Judges 11:19-22 Jephthah refers to this last event, and centuries later King Mesha of Moab told how, thanks to his god Chemosh, he freed himself from Israelite domination around 850 B.C. The area earlier conquered by Sihon had now been taken in turn by Israel as far as Dibon and Medeba and, according to verse 32, all the way to Jazer. The song recited by the bards now ends as a song of victory for Israel.

OG OF BASHAN 21:33–22:1

After the conquest of the land of Sihon, Israel marched north toward the fruitful territory of Og, king of Bashan, a land that bordered to the south on the Jabbok and to the north on the Yarmuk area by the Sea of Galilee. The Israelites had not engaged in any military action against the Ammonites on their right because, like the Moabites and the Edomites, they were related to them. The Lord had given this land to them and not to the Israelites (see Deut. 2:5, 9, 19).

There is no mention of any request to be allowed to pass through Bashan. No transaction of any kind is said to have taken place. The people simply went into battle at Edrei by the northern river, the Yarmuk. Og, together with his sons and army, was crushingly defeated—and that despite the fact that according to Deuteronomy 3:11, Og belonged to the dreaded family of giants called the Rephaim. In verse 34 we read that

God told Moses to set aside fear: with battle as with all things, the people had to receive his instructions in a spirit of trust. And indeed he decided the issue in their favor as he said he would, giving Og into the power of Israel. Thus this event joined the series of mighty acts the Lord accomplished. In Nehemiah 9:22 and Psalms 135:10-12 and 136:17-22, both Sihon and Og are mentioned in one breath as dreaded kings that were wiped out by the God of Israel. Here, on the east side of the Jordan, the people got a taste of what they could expect to happen on the west side—if they maintained faith and trust in their Lord.

THE SUMMONING OF BALAAM 22:2-21

After conquering the territories of Sihon and Og, Israel's troops came together and camped north of the Dead Sea by the Jordan; viewed from the west side, that would have been over against Jericho. Balak, king of Moab, felt very threatened by this development, and so he went out to seek support from the Midianites, a nomadic people who wandered around in the steppes to the east and south. The Targum Pseudo-Jonathan offers the information that the two nations had some kind of special union in which each provided a king in turn. Whatever the case, the Moabites and the Midianites acted in concert, although from this point on we hear very little about Midian.

Moab did not feel strong enough militarily to meet the threat. Another method was needed to break the power of the adversary: the power-filled word of one who was endowed with supernatural gifts. Egyptians had long used the magic words of their so-called imprecatory texts, and Goliath cursed David before proceeding to attack him (1 Sam. 17:43-44). The man whom Balak judged to be able to curse effectively was Balaam, son of Beor, at Pethor. Pethor is usually associated with Pitru by the Euphrates (called Pedru by the Egyptians). The word translated as "his people" in the KJV is translated in the RSV as a proper name—Amaw, a city in northern Syria. The Samaritan text and the Vulgate read "Ammon." In view of the distance between the Euphrates River and the neighborhood of Jericho, there is much to be said for this last reading. Nearby Ammon would make more sense with regard to the story of the donkey (vv. 22-25), since such an animal would not have been a preferred form of transportation on a long journey.

The elders of Moab and Midian, as Balak's messengers, went to Balaam with the fees for divination in their hands, the reward for the curses he was to pronounce. As is evident from 1 Samuel 9:8, 1 Kings 13:7 and 14:3, and 2 Kings 5:5, it was natural even in Israel to bring along a gift for the man of God. The elders, called "princes" (vv. 8ff.; a better term would be "dignitaries"), brought the message to Balaam.

The first element of the message was the formal opening—"Thus says Balak, son of Zippor." This was followed by a rehearsal of the circumstances that led to the sending of an embassy: a people had come out of Egypt so huge that they covered the face of the earth. Finally, there was a request: Come to Moab and from there pronounce a curse on this people. When that is done, the deadly threat would be removed, and "perhaps [one cannot be entirely sure, after all] I shall be able to fight against them and drive them from the land."

Balaam refused to answer immediately; he invited the messengers to stay the night so that he might have time to learn from God his will in the situation. The story of what occurred that night makes one think of 1 Samuel 3:4-10, in which we read that the Lord called the young Samuel and gave him an assignment. In Numbers 22:9 we read that God appeared to Balaam, asking him about the men who had come as messengers. Balaam replied by repeating their message and asking God to come along and curse Israel. God's command in response was, "You shall not go with them; you shall not curse the people, for they are blessed." There could be no question of cursing them. The next morning Balaam passed on the words of God, emphatically underscoring the fact that the Lord would not let him go to curse Israel. The translation of the Targum here uses a phrase we also encounter in Matthew 11:26 and 18:14: "It is not the good pleasure before the Lord to let me go with you." This was not quite what the messengers transmitted according to verse 14. They did not say that the Lord refused but rather that Balaam refused to go along. No wonder Balak felt that he only had to impress Balaam a bit more to persuade him to come. In any case, he sent a bigger embassy, consisting of more important men with greater powers to "honor" him—which usually meant "to offer a bigger honorarium"; indeed, Balaam could name his own price if only he would come to curse Israel.

We might expect that at this point the soothsayer-prophet would simply have sent the messengers home. There had been no change in God's command: Israel remained a blessed people. But a certain ambivalence is evident in Balaam's behavior. Verse 18 would seem to suggest that he was adamant: no matter how much he was offered, he said, he would never do anything against the will of God—not for all the treasure in the king's house. But still he allowed the messengers to stay overnight. Again he expected to hear from the Lord. Did he imagine that God would have changed his mind so that he might yet pronounce a curse on the people from the desert and get the full honorarium? This is how the matter is presented in 2 Peter 2:15 and Jude 11, in which he is pictured as one who loved the wages of wickedness.

And indeed, verse 20 seems to indicate that God did change his mind. He gave permission to Balaam to go along—but only on the condition that he say no more than what the Lord would give him to say. This might seem to have opened the way to fulfilling both the desire of Balak and the secret wishes of Balaam. But verses 22-35 indicate that this was definitely not the case. This passage shows how God sovereignly carries out his plan regardless of any human schemes.

As is evident from long passages in the Targum Pseudo-Jonathan, later Jewish writers put Balaam in a very bad light. The Hebrew text indicates that this non-Israelite used the name "Lord"—even spoke of "the Lord, my God"—and also that he shrank from doing anything against the will of God, but the Targum does not have a single good word to say about him. It puts him on a level with Laban, who ill-treated the children of his daughters, and his name is said to mean "devourer of people." In connection with 22:30 the Targum charges him with bestiality, and in connection with 31:8 it describes how he used the most outlandish magical means to escape Phinehas the priest. Is it not better to say that there were two sides to the man? On the one hand, he wanted to subject his will to that of God and say only what the Lord ordered him to say, whatever the consequences. On the other hand, he also desired "the reward of unrighteousness." But in any case, if God employs an individual in his service, then something has to happen in that person's life. In Numbers 22:22-35 we find what happened in Balaam's life.

THE DUMB ANIMAL TALKS 22:22-35

This passage is a clearly constructed whole. It presupposes that Balaam made a journey through open fields and between vineyards with narrow passageways—which makes perfect sense in the Trans-Jordan area.

It is somewhat surprising to read in verse 22 that the Lord's anger was kindled, since he had just given his permission for the trip. Not until verse 32 does it become clear why he should have placed himself in opposition to the soothsayer-prophet: the path the man had chosen would end in his own destruction. How can people seek both to do God's will and to follow their own wrong desires? With severity the Lord forced him to choose a single course of action. The messengers of Balak show up again only in verse 35. The two young servants, called Jannes and Jambres by the Targum Pseudo-Jonathan (cf. 2 Tim. 3:8), do not play much of a role in the story. The entire focus seems to be on Balaam. Whereas the donkey could see the angel of the Lord, the eyes of the soothsayer-prophet were strangely blind. There is a kind of movement toward a climax both in the events and in the conversations.

First, the animal turned off the road and into the open field and Balaam beat her to get her back on the road. Next the angel positioned himself on a narrow path between two vineyards walls, and the donkey tried to get around him. The animal pressed closely against one wall, crushing Balaam's foot in the process. A second beating followed. Finally, the angel took a position where the path was so narrow that the animal could not possibly pass by him, and so she lay down. Balaam was so furious that he gave her yet another beating.

From numerous examples in the culture of Mesopotamia and Egypt, we know that soothsayers could infer things having to do with the supernatural world from unusual animal behavior. If Balaam belonged to their guild, we have to say that in this case he completely misread the behavior of his mount. Only a divine intervention could give him true insight.

The same point is made with the dialogue. First the donkey asked why he beat her and the answer was, "Because you have made sport of me." Then she asked whether she deserved this kind of behavior in light of the fact that she had served him faithfully all his life, and he granted that she did not. That pointed to the fact that something unusual was involved here, something the donkey could not make clear to him. Only God could. So the passage climaxes in the decisive words of verse 31: "the Lord opened the eyes of Balaam"—literally, "he removed the scales from his eyes." Only then did Balaam see the whole scene: the angel of the Lord who was threatening him with death on account of his conduct. No wonder Balaam showed extreme reverence toward the angel, confessing his sin and vowing to turn back. Of course this put him in a new predicament. He knew that on pain of death he would have to abide by the command to say only the words the Lord put in his mouth.

Between verse 22 and verse 35, both of which say the same thing, there lies a world of divine depth. God goes his own majestic way through history. If necessary he will use dumb animals to warn his prophets and open the eyes of those who think they can see everything. The Lord's plan for his people and his world is accomplished.

BALAK MEETS BALAAM 22:36-40

The "city of Moab" must have been situated somewhere near the Arnon. It was the meeting place for Balaam coming from the north and Balak coming from the south. The king was annoyed by Balaam's late arrival. Was this how he responded to the summons of a king? Did the soothsayer-prophet not think that the king would be able to reward him adequately? Balaam responded to the criticism by simply pointing out that he had in fact arrived. Beyond that he warned that he could not say a thing. He was completely dependent on the words God would give him to say. This was to control the ensuing course of events completely.

From the city of Moab they traveled together in a northerly direction toward the steppes where the Israelites were camped, to Kiriath-huzoth, the city of streets. There the king ordered that oxen and sheep be butchered and that the roast meat be served to Balaam and the dignitaries who were with him. Important events were often ushered in by a common meal, which was intended to strengthen mutual ties. Such of course was Balak's intent in this instance.

THE FIRST ORACLE 22:41–23:12

First thing in the morning Balak took Balaam with him to Bamoth-baal, a place name meaning "Heights of Baal" (see

22:41, NEB). These may have been ordinary hilltops, but it is more likely they were holy heights, sacred to such deities as Nebo, Peor, and Baal.

From the elevation of Bamoth-baal they could see the outer fringe of the army camps of Israel, situated down in the steppes by the Jordan River. In order to lay a spell on a people, it was considered necessary to be able to see them, if only in part.

As part of the preparations, there had to be a sacrifice—the grander the better. On Balaam's instructions, Balak, acting for his people, used seven altars, sacrificing on each in turn a bull and a ram as an "offering to God's majesty," a sign of submission and surrender to God. The king and his officials remained by the altars as Balaam went off in hopes of receiving a revelation from God. His words in verse 3 imply that this was not something he could take for granted. It all depended on the graciousness of the Lord. In respectful expectation, the soothsayer-prophet went to a place referred to as "a barren height" elsewhere in the Old Testament. The ancient versions offer a variety of renderings. The Septuagint says that he "went straight" to ask God. The Targum Onkelos says that he went "alone." The Targum Neofiti says that he went "calmly, quietly." The Targum Pseudo-Jonathan says that he went "as a snake." The Vulgate says that he went "quickly." In any case, the Lord did grant Balaam a revelation. He received a message to pass on to Balak. As a prophet transmitting the voice of God, he had to begin by saying, "Thus says the Lord."

We have received the divine answer in poetic form, which indicates that it had the authority of an oracle. The text appears in parallel clauses, and we sometimes have to infer the meaning of its words from their synonyms in the parallel lines.

Balaam described how he was brought from Aram. His task was *to curse, to utter imprecations over, to denounce* Israel—all terms that indicate how one can break a people with words. But, one may ask, was that humanly possible? To go against the will of God? To curse where he blesses? In the promise to Abraham there was reference to descendants as numerous as the sand by the sea and the stars in the heavens. Now Balak could see with his own eyes, even from a distance, signs of how large Israel had become. Verse 10a mentions the dust of Jacob, but we are less certain of the meaning of the term in 10b, though we can safely assume that it must mean something similar because of the parallel sentence structure. As the note to the verse in the RSV suggests, it may mean "dust cloud" (there is a related word in Assyrian-Babylonian with that meaning): dust cannot be numbered, nor can the particles of a dust cloud. The preferred translation, however, is "the fourth part," which conveys the idea that even a fourth of Israel's army is beyond numbering, much less the people as a whole.

According to verse 9 the people were not only innumerable, but they also had a unique position. It was not just one nation among many. It was an elect people, God's special possession, belonging to him alone. It was precisely this that made Balaam—an outsider, a foreigner—wish he might share in the life and death of the righteous. According to the Targum Pseudo-Jonathan, he said, "If only I were as one of the least of them." He expressed his desire to meet the same end they did. Some scholars translate the term in verse 10b not as "end" but as "descendants," understanding the text to mean that he wished his descendants might share in the blessing of the Israelites. These words make it clear how the oracle is charged through and through with blessing rather than cursing.

It is no wonder that Balak, in utter consternation, demanded to know what Balaam was doing to him. He had been called to strike Israel with his curses, but he delivered nothing but blessing. Balaam responded by underscoring the most essential point of the oracle: it is not the will of Balak or Balaam that decides anything; only the pronouncement of the Lord has such power.

THE SECOND ORACLE 23:13-26

After the failure of the first attempt to put a curse on Israel, Balak brought Balaam to another location for another attempt. They went somewhat farther to the north, to the top of Mount Pisgah. As is evident from the name "the field of watchers" (Zophim), it was a place from which a good view of the surrounding area could be obtained.

It is not clear what the exact significance of Balak's statement that Balaam would see "the nearest" of the Israelites but not all of them (v. 13) might be, but it seems likely that this new vantage point at least allowed them to see a larger portion of the people than had been visible at Bamoth-baal. The same preparations were made here as had been made on the first occasion: seven altars were set up, and a bull and a ram were sacrificed on each. The king and his officials remained by the altars. Balaam went away to meet God and then returned with the divine answer.

We have received this communication, too, in poetic form. It begins with lines that stress the great difference between God and man. Human beings sometimes lie, sometimes speak of their intention to do things that in fact they never manage to accomplish. Such is not the case with God. He never lies, and hence he never has any cause to repent; moreover, he accomplishes everything that it is his will to accomplish. The idea of God "repenting" does occur elsewhere in the Old Testament, however, and it is clearly a difficult concept. The Septuagint handles such passages by substituting various terms and phrases for the Hebrew term meaning "repent." Indeed, even here, where the text explicitly states that God has no need to repent, the Septuagint substitutes a term meaning that he would not "let himself be dissuaded." The Targums omit the words relating to God altogether in this context, saying only that he is not unreliable or unstable like people are. On the contrary, we can depend on him unconditionally. But God is not all rigid and unfeeling majesty. Genesis 6:6 indicates that he reacted to the entire range of human conduct by bringing judgment on the world; Jonah 3:10 provides an example of his reacting in mercy toward Nineveh. In the end, then, if we are to use the word "repentance" with respect to God, we must remember that it is not the same as *human* repentance. Numbers 23:19 underscores that point emphatically, as does 1 Samuel 15:29. Balaam wanted Balak to know in no uncertain terms that sacrifices, magical practices, and the employment of famous soothsayers would not serve to bring about a change of mind in God.

According to verse 20, the message Balaam received from the Lord was all blessing. It flowed like a river upon this people—irresistibly. Its content was reproduced in two words: "no misfortune," "no misery" (v. 21, NIV). God's blessing means prosperity, well-being, peace. The reason, according to verse 21b, was that the Lord was their God, bound to them by covenant. The phrase "the shout of a king is among them" in 21b has been variously interpreted. The Targum Onkelos speaks of the indwelling of the Lord here, making the phrase a strict parallel of the preceding phrase. But the reference is to a king who is being celebrated. Who is this king? A ruler (as the

Septuagint suggests)? A Messiah (as the Targum Pseudo-Jonathan has it)? There is much to be said for the messianic option. It was God's power that had to that point led Israel out of Egypt, and he promised to continue to lead his people. Verse 22 includes an image from Egypt and Mesopotamia to underscore that promise—the wild ox, which thrusts down everything in its path with its fearful horns.

The statement recorded in verse 23 makes it plain that nothing can stop the progress of the people. The preposition preceding the words Jacob and Israel can be translated "in" (as is the case in the Targums and the NEB), in which case the text would mean that there was no form of sorcery, divination, or magic in Israel. But such a reading is problematic, because the biblical record contradicts it. The fact is that there was sorcery in Israel. The first king, Saul, and one of the last, Josiah, both fought against those who consulted the dead—in vain it would seem. The prophets repeatedly charged the people with participation in all kinds of dark practices. So in the end it seem wiser to translate the preposition as "against" (as in the RSV and NIV), in which case the passage would be indicating that neither sorcery nor divination would have any negative impact on this people.

Israel was not vulnerable; to the contrary, it was like a lioness or a lion (v. 24). The lion does not lie down to rest until the prey has been eaten and the blood has all been drunk. This people was invincible, to be dreaded. The Targums, going beyond the imagery to the matter itself, say that Israel would not rest till it had slaughtered the nations and taken possession of their wealth. The nation's strength came not from itself, however, but from God. Verse 23b speaks of what God had done for his people, a theme picked up in Romans 8:37 as well: they were more than conquerors through him.

Not surprisingly, Balak was once more upset by the continued blessing of his enemies. If you don't want to curse the people, then at least refrain from blessing them, he pleaded. To which Balaam once more replied, "Did I not tell you, 'All that the Lord says, that I must do.'"

THE THIRD ORACLE 23:27–24:13

After a second failure, Balak again tried to reach his goal by choosing a third elevation—the top of Peor, from which they could get a view of all the Israelites. The previous locations at which the sacrifices had been offered and from which Balaam delivered his oracles probably lay further to the north. We shall have to imagine that the first time around the soothsayer-prophet only saw a narrow edge of the armed camp, the second time a wider strip, and the third time all the Israelites in their separate tribal encampments. Balak made the same preparations on the third occasion, though with a bit more modesty (v. 27: "perhaps it will please God").

There was a change in Balaam's conduct on this third attempt. It was not his intent to secure his goal by magical means, described in 24:1 as "meet[ing] with omens" (RSV) or "sorcery" (NIV), a practice which sometimes involved the use of snakes. Nor did he count on a revelation from God as he had before. No, this time everything proceeded from God: the Spirit of God came over Balaam (v. 2) and he began to see things that were hidden to others and hear words of which others had no knowledge. Overpowered, he fell prostrate on the ground (v. 4). The expression "whose eye is opened" in verse 3 can also be translated "whose eye is closed" (see the note to the verse in the RSV). In any case, he sees in a vision with unclouded eye what God gives, and will give, his people.

In poetic language that is very difficult to translate in some passages, this oracle contains Balaam's description of how abundantly the Lord bestowed his blessings on Israel. It starts in verse 5 with a doxology on the dwellings of the people. They were like extended river valleys, like gardens situated by a river (Targum Onkelos reads "the Euphrates"), like aloes planted by the Lord, like cedars usually seen in Lebanon but standing by water here. In short, the scene was altogether splendid. Verse 7a refers to the great fertility of the land as a result of a plentiful supply of water. In a land that is often dry, moisture means everything; seed sown in wet ground carries within it the promise of a rich harvest.

The Septuagint has a very different text, referring to someone who would come forth from the seed of Israel as a ruler. This ties in with verse 7b, where there is mention of a king of Israel who would be greater than Agag. Is this perhaps a reference to Saul who slew the Amalekites (1 Sam. 15)? Or is Agag a royal title like "Pharaoh"? Or is it Gog (as the Samaritan text and the Septuagint have it), a figure of the end time in Ezekiel 38-39? If this last is the case, then the text has messianic implications. Verses 8 and 9 describe in graphic terms how formidable the people will be. It will devour its adversaries and break their bones in pieces. It will be as irresistibly powerful as the lion and the lioness. No sensible person would risk provoking these dangerous predatory animals. Israel would have the strength of these animals—though it would not come from the people. As verse 8a stresses, all their power derived from God. God's people had its identity only because God delivered them from Egypt, still delivered them, and would continue to deliver them (cf. 2 Cor. 1:10). Those who blessed this people would themselves be blessed; those who cursed them would be cursed.

After the third oracle, Balak's patience was exhausted. With a gesture (v. 10: "he struck his hands together") that may have expressed horror, anger, or contempt, he dismissed Balaam without any payment. He blamed his failure to provide an honorarium on God: "the Lord has kept you from being rewarded" (v. 11, NIV). The soothsayer-prophet answered that he had simply been faithful to his word. He had said from the beginning that as a true prophet he could do no more than transmit the word of the Lord, regardless of what might happen to himself.

THE FOURTH ORACLE 24:14-19

Before returning to his own people, Balaam gave yet another bit of advice to Balak concerning the future of his people, apparently in order to warn the Moabite king against impulsive and hasty actions, for Balaam had seen that the king would not be able to stand up to the people whose life was lived under God's blessing. The oracle is composed in poetic phrases in parallel constructions: "him who hears," "[him who] knows the knowledge," "[him] who sees the vision"; and "God," "the Most High," "the Almighty." Fallen prostrate (or "fallen into sleep," as the Septuagint has it), Balaam saw someone far away in time ("not now") and space ("not nigh"). This person was to appear like a star and rise like a scepter. This future ruler would rise out of Israel to strike down the Moabites. The Shethites ("the sons of Sheth," v. 17), a nomadic people known from Egyptian texts as the Sutu, would experience the same fate. The Samaritan text offers clear parallels between "the foreheads of Moab" and "the skulls of the Shethites." The third people that would be subdued and robbed of its land was Edom. Some ancient versions, passing from image to reality, refer to the extermination of the leaders and numbers of the subjugated nations.

Who was Balaam referring to here? Obviously not to a contemporary, for he pointed to the future. On the basis of 2 Samuel 8:1-14 we might think David a good candidate. But there is another, more compelling possibility. There are messianic expectations connected with the symbols of "star" and "scepter," as the various Targums make clear. Targum Onkelos reads "king," "messiah"; Targum Neofiti reads "redeemer," "ruler"; Targum Pseudo-Jonathan reads "king," "messiah." Much later, the Jews called the leader of an uprising against the Romans in A.D. 132-35 Bar-Kochba—"Son of the Star"— plainly a messianic title. The Targum Pseudo-Jonathan refers even to Rome, Constantinople, and Caesarea-by-the-Sea. The New Testament also contains a number of references to the star (e.g., Luke 1:78; Rev. 22:16) in which the subject is Jesus, the Christ.

THREE ORACLES: THE CONCLUSION 24:20-25

Verses 20-25 contain three final oracles which conclude the story of Balaam and Balak and bring the total number of oracles to seven, a symbol of wholeness or completeness.

Verse 20 refers to the nomadic tribe of the Amalekites who wandered in the desert area of the Negeb. According to Exodus 17:8-16, Israel fought with the Amalekites. We read in 1 Samuel 15:7-9 that King Saul fought them, and 1 Samuel 27:8 tells us that David also fought them. As this passage points out, this people obviously had some importance, but it had no future.

Verses 21-22 concern the Kenites, descendants of Kain, a people who lived in rock fortresses southwest of the Dead Sea. Although their "nest" (a play on the word Kain in Hebrew) appears to be uncapturable, it will nevertheless be destroyed by another nomadic people, the Asshurites, who lived somewhere in the north of the Sinai peninsula. In verse 23, the Septuagint mentions Og, but the reference is unclear. Verse 24 mentions two nations: Asshur and Eber. The first comprises the nomads referred to in verse 22. Eber is less clear. Perhaps it was another nomadic people or a group related to Israel (Eber = Hebrews?). Whatever the case, both of these tribes were to be subdued and humiliated by the men of Kittim, named after the city of Kition on Cyprus. In the end all of these oppressors would be vanquished.

Later interpreters came to understand the names in verses 20-24 as identifying not small nations but greater political entities. Some equated Asshur with the mighty nation of the Assyrians, Eber with the region beyond the Euphrates, and the people of Kittim with the entire Greek world at the time of Alexander the Great. Still later, these names were applied to the successors of Alexander and finally even to the Romans. The Targum Pseudo-Jonathan mentions ships from Liburnia in northern Italy in conjunction with troops connected with the armies of Rome and Constantinople. The Qumran sect did the same with other texts of the Old Testament, reading contemporary history back into the ancient names.

In any event, verse 23b contains the core of the whole passage: when God intervenes, who can remain on his feet? In due time, every conqueror is swept aside by him. Whether the references are to nomadic tribes or world empires, the Messiah-king has the last word.

BAAL OF PEOR 25:1-5

When the Israelites arrived at Shittim, they were situated close to the crossing of the Jordan. There they came in contact with the Moabites and their religion. The women of Moab achieved what Balak could not. They invited the Israelites to take part in a community meal in honor of the local deity, the Baal of Peor, which served to establish close ties between the deity and those who took part in the community sacrifice. One of the aspects of this sacrificial worship was ritual sexual intercourse with the women. For the Israelite men who partook in the rite, it constituted not only literal fornication (unfaithfulness to their wives) but also religious fornication—unfaithfulness to the Lord.

In response to this open infidelity, the Lord became very angry. According to verse 4 he commanded Moses to arrest all the chiefs of Israel and execute them. The word designating the means of execution is not clear; it is variously translated as "hanging," "impalement," and even "being tossed off a cliff." In any case, the execution was to be carried out publicly—literally, "over against the sun." This punishment, which is also prescribed in 2 Samuel 21:6-9, was apparently judged to have expiatory force. The chiefs were evidently held to be responsible for the conduct of the people, and as their representatives they had to atone for their sin. The command Moses gave (v. 5) was different: he charged the judges (or the tribes, as the Septuagint and the Samaritan text have it) to execute those who were actually guilty. The text does not say in what way the verdict had to be carried out. Only after the punishment had been carried out did the anger of God abate.

THE FERTILITY CULT 25:6-18

Whereas verses 1-5 report that Moabite women seduced the Israelites into serving other gods, in verses 6-18 the reference is to a distinguished Midianite woman who played an important role. The remark in verse 6 concerning the weeping Israelites may refer to the heavy blow that had struck them, but it seems more likely that it is a reference to a practice associated with a pagan fertility cult that was popular throughout the ancient Near Eastern world. In Ezekiel 8:14 we read that the prophet saw women mourning for the Mesopotamian fertility god Tammuz.

The story of what happens to Zimri, a noted leader of the tribe of Simeon, is also open to two interpretations. Some scholars contend that Zimri brought Cozbi, the daughter of a Midianite chief, to the tent of his brothers in order to take her publicly as his wife, in full view of Moses and all the people. The Targum Pseudo-Jonathan indicates that he silenced Moses' objections to the marriage by pointing out that Moses had himself taken a Midianite woman to be his wife. The second interpretation of Zimri's conduct with Cozbi is that he was engaging in further worship of the Baal of Peor, that he was carrying out the rites of the fertility cult with the Midianite woman. It was the assumption of the cult that the fertility of people, cattle, and crops depended on the sexual linkage of a god and goddess. By imitating this union of the gods, men and women would seek to induce the gods to grant a greater measure of fertility. Such cultic practices were common in all of the nations surrounding the Israelites. Obviously, some Israelites did not want to be excepted. At this point, when Israel was about to enter the promised land, Israel proved to have more confidence in the power of foreign gods than in the omnipotence of the Lord. The people spurned his glory and uniqueness. So we need not be surprised when we read in verse 11 that his jealousy was aroused. He was for Israel the Only One. Again, the second interpretation seems the more convincing. Zimri's act constituted a denial of God's very being.

It was in this context that Phinehas, the grandson of Aaron, was moved to take the exceptionally rigorous action he did. He saw in Zimri's act a threat to the whole of Israel. If the people of Israel continued on this road, they would disappear from the face of the earth. For that reason he followed the two offenders into the tent and killed them both with a single spear thrust. The Targum Pseudo-Jonathan offers the information that the two were struck simultaneously in the lower part of their bodies and presents a graphic and gruesome (even fantastic) description of what took place. People were obviously deeply impressed by this event for centuries. This is evident not just from a story of twelve miraculous signs that were said to have been revealed here but also from artistic representations of the event that have been uncovered by archeologists.

According to verses 8-9, Phinehas's action brought to an end a plague that had to that point taken 24,000 lives. Doubtless it is his act that is being referred to in verse 13c, which says that "atonement" was made. Altogether, then, this passage gives us a list of three executions: that of the chiefs (v. 4), that of the guilty parties (v. 5), and that of Zimri and Cozbi (v. 8). There must be atonement for sin.

Phinehas's action had other consequences for himself and his descendants as well. The foundation of genuine priesthood is the attitude one assumes toward God. Only one whose life is centered in God can perform the tasks of the priesthood. And so it was that God made "a covenant of peace" (a phrase that can also be translated "my covenant which embraces peace") with Phinehas. But the essential requirement of the priesthood underscored here points to the fact that in the end there is only one who can be a true priest—Jesus Christ.

THE CENSUS 26:1-51

The order in which the names of the patriarchs are listed in this passage deviates somewhat from that in Genesis 29:31–30:24. In connection with the distribution of the land, the tribe of Levi is treated separately. The census involves all able-bodied men twenty years old and older. Table 1 compares the figures listed for the census reported in this chapter with those given for the census reported in chapter 1.

TABLE 1

The names of the tribes	Numbers ch. 1	Numbers ch. 26	the difference
Reuben	46,500	43,730	− 2,770
Simeon	59,300	22,200	−37,100
Gad	45,650	40,500	− 5,150
Judah	74,600	76,500	+ 1,900
Issachar	54,400	64,300	+ 9,900
Zebulun	57,400	60,500	+ 3,100
Ephraim	40,500	32,500	− 8,000
Manasseh	32,200	52,700	+20,500
Benjamin	35,400	45,600	+10,200
Dan	62,700	64,400	+ 1,700
Asher	41,500	53,400	+11,900
Naphtali	53,400	45,400	− 8,000
TOTAL	603,550	601,730	− 1,820

The census in chapter 1 took place in the second month of the second year after the exodus; the census in chapter 26 took place approximately thirty-eight years later, shortly before the entry. The final figures vary only slightly. Some tribes changed little in size; others, quite a lot. Simeon for instance, lost a lot, and Manasseh increased a lot.

A number of additions interrupt the well-ordered summaries of tribes and clans. In verses 9-11 we read of the three sons of Eliab, two of whom—Dathan and Abiram—we recall from chapter 16. As noted in verses 9-10, Korah, Dathan, and Abiram were swallowed by the earth, while the 250 leading men were consumed by fire. Verse 11 tells us that the line of Korah did not die out, however. According to the Targum Pseudo-Jonathan they did not consent to their father's plan, but followed the instructions of Moses. It is on the basis of this information that we can explain the existence of the guild of Korahite singers.

In verse 21 the two names of the sons of Perez are added to the line of Judah-Perez.

Verses 29-33 provide a description of the line of Manasseh that is much more detailed than that of any of the other tribes: Manasseh's son Machir had a son Gilead, and Gilead had seven sons. The line of one of Gilead's sons, Hepher, is continued: he had a son, Zelophehad, who in turn had five daughters. From this long genealogy we can conclude the following: Manasseh was old enough to have experienced the good days in Egypt. Zelophehad died in the wilderness after the rebellion of Korah and his following. Machir, Gilead, Hepher, and Zelophehad must all have personally experienced the oppression of Egypt—four successive generations. On the basis of this evidence we can conclude that the period of slavery must have lasted about a hundred years.

Verses 36, 40, and 45 also amplify the list of descendants somewhat. Verse 46 mentions the name of Serah, a daughter of Asher; the Targum Pseudo-Jonathan tells the story of how Serah was transported by many thousands of angels into the garden of Eden yet during her lifetime. Verses 42-43 would seem to suggest that Dan had only one son, and that all of his descendants, described as very numerous in Numbers, were descendants of just that one.

THE ALLOTMENT OF THE LAND 26:52-56

These verses clearly show the purpose of the census: it provided a basis for the fair distribution of the land that the Lord had given to his people. Every tribe would have its own piece of land. Verse 54 indicates that the size of the tribe's population was to determine the size of its inheritance. But then verse 55 states that the inheritances are to be determined by lot. Verse 56 clarifies the apparent contradiction: the size of the tribe will determine the size of the area of their inheritance, and the lot will determine the position of the inheritance allotted.

THE CENSUS OF THE LEVITES: CONCLUSION 26:57-65

Verses 57-62 provide a separate accounting of the tribe of Levites, using different standards. They constituted a different case because they were not to receive an allotment of land as their inheritance and they were not candidates for military service in the literal sense. Moses and Eleazar counted all males among them one month old and older. At the census in the wilderness of Sinai their number was 22,000; at the census on the plains of Moab, some thirty-eight years later, it was 23,000—1,000 more.

There are two clan lists. One shows the names of Gershon, Kohath, and Merari (v. 57); the other shows the names of Libni, Hebron, Mahli, Mushi, and Korah. All these names occur elsewhere in Numbers 3, 4, and 16 in different contexts. We shall have to assume that there were different lists in circulation, each with its own kind of validity. From the remarkable parenthesis in verses 59-61 we find that the line of priests descended from Amram, the son of Kohath, and Jochebed, the sister of Kohath. Such a union was evidently permitted in ancient times, though after the time Leviticus 18:12 and 20:19 were written, it was clearly no longer allowed.

Finally, verses 63-65 tell us that by the time of this second census, none of those registered at the first census was still living except Caleb and Joshua, a fact that is in keeping with the word of God. A completely new generation would enter the land.

THE INHERITANCE RIGHTS OF DAUGHTERS 27:1-11

This passage presents a situation similar to those described in Numbers 9:1-14; 15:32-36; and 36:1-9. A problem came up and was laid before the leaders; when they could not provide a solution, they took it to the Lord for a decision. His pronouncement established the rule and fixed it for the future.

From Numbers 27:1-11 we may infer the following. Only sons had the right to inherit. In the absence of male issue, the inheritance passed to male members of the man's clan in a certain predetermined order. It is also clear from verse 3 that a man who committed flagrant crimes would forfeit his inheritance, and it would no longer pass to his children. An example of such a crime is the rebellion of Korah and his following.

In the case of the five daughters of Zelophehad, there were no sons, and the law demanded that his inheritance pass to male relatives. There was no question of forfeiture, because he was not involved with the rebellious group under Korah and had not committed any other crimes. But in effect, the law called for the end of his family line because it treated daughters as if they did not exist. If his inheritance should fall to male relatives, his name would disappear from Israel's ranks.

For these reasons, the five daughters came before Moses, Eleazar, the leaders of the people, and the entire community to request that the inheritance be given to them as legal heirs.

Without precedent to draw on, Moses turned to the Lord for a decision. The answer was favorable to the daughters. They could receive their father's inheritance—and Joshua 17:3-6 informs us that they did in fact receive it.

Following this decision, a new set of rules for inheritance was established. As verses 8-11 indicate, sons were to retain first rights to any inheritance. If there were no sons, the daughters would become the heirs. If the deceased had no children at all, his brothers would inherit. If there were no brothers, the claim to possession of the inheritance would move back a generation to the father's brothers. In the absence of such brothers, the nearest relative would receive the inheritance.

Behind this ruling lay the idea that inherited possessions—specifically land—always had to remain in the same family circle within the same clan. After all, every tribe, every clan, and every family had to live off the soil, and it was only through the link with inherited possessions that the name of the deceased would be perpetuated.

A SUCCESSOR TO MOSES 27:12-23

In verses 12-14 we read that the Lord commanded Moses to climb the Abarim mountain range. The Septuagint reads "the mountain that is on the other side of the Jordan, Mount Nebo." From that vantage point one could view the whole of Canaan. After embracing the promised land with his gaze, which is an act of possession of sorts from a distance, he would die. The phrase "to be gathered to your people" may originally have been a reference to entering the family grave, but here it has an ironic meaning, for Moses was in fact to go off alone, away from his fellowmen. In this connection, the Lord referred to the events surrounding "the water of contention" (RSV, "waters of Meribah") at Kadesh.

No complaint crossed Moses' lips (vv. 15-17). He did not refer to himself at all. All that occupied him was the idea of caring for the future of his people. As in Numbers 16:22, we read the he addressed the Lord as "the God of the spirits of all flesh." The Targum Pseudo-Jonathan reads "the Word of the Lord that rules the breath of mankind and from whom spirit and breath are given to all flesh." The Septuagint reads "the God of the spirits and of all flesh." Moses' prayer was marked by a thorough reverence, a sense of dependence on and trust in the Creator, who would not forsake the work of his hands. Moses asked him for a man to "go out before [the people] and come in before them," someone to "lead them out and bring them in"—expressions that refer to military actions. And indeed, as the people entered the new land they were going to need an able commander to ensure the fulfillment of the promise. Without a good and forceful commander, the people would be as defenseless as a flock of sheep without a shepherd.

We read of the answer to Moses' prayer in verses 18-20. The Lord appointed Joshua, the son of Nun, to be Moses' successor. Already in chapters 13 and 14 it is noted that there was a special spirit in him. Caleb and Joshua were different from the other spies. God directed Moses to take him from the people and lay his hands on him, thereby symbolically laying the burden of leadership on him. Next Moses was to place him before Eleazar and the entire assembly and commission him in full view of the people. Finally he was to invest Joshua with some of his own authority, something that can best be understood as a charisma that induced in all the people a readiness to listen to him with confidence.

Verses 21-23 point out a difference between Moses and Joshua. Moses had enjoyed a unique place before the Lord and spoken with him face to face, but Joshua was to learn the will of God through Eleazar. The Urim was to play a key role in this new process of revelation. Scholars are not entirely certain what the Urim was, but apparently it was composed of two staffs or stones, one which one meant Yes and the other No. They would be shaken in an oracle bag or jar, and the stone that fell out would be taken as an indication of the divine answer. In conducting military operations this was an important matter. In all cases the lot was the oracle that decided (see 1 Sam. 23:9-13; 30:7-8). The Targum Pseudo-Jonathan on Numbers 27:21b reads, "And he shall minister before Eleazar the priest; and when any matter is hidden from him, he shall inquire for him before the Lord by Uraia. According to the word of Eleazar the priest they shall go forth to battle, and come in to do judgment, he, and all the sons of Israel with him, even all the congregation." That means Joshua was to be totally dependent on the guidance God gave him through the intermediation of the priest. That placed the surrender of the land completely in his hands and ensured that the future would be secure so long as the people continued to walk in the obedience of faith.

THE DAILY OFFERING TO GOD'S MAJESTY 28:1-8

According to verse 6, the specifications for the offering to God's majesty were set out at Mount Sinai. Three related sacrifices had to be brought twice daily (cf. Exod. 29:38-42), once in the morning and once at twilight. The Targum Pseudo-Jonathan tells us that this was to expiate the sins of the night and those of the past day.

The one offering had the character of acknowledging and submitting to the majesty of God. It consisted of a year-old male lamb. The second offering, often linked with the first and similarly expressive of submission and surrender, was the homage offering. It consisted of about two quarts of fine flour, mixed with about one quart of beaten olive oil. The third offering was a libation or drink offering. It consisted of about one quart of fermented drink (v. 7). The parallel text (Exod. 29:40) mentions wine. All three were meant to express a sense of dependence on the Lord.

The animal and cereal offerings can be called the food of God, and the libations the drink of God—but only in a figurative sense, of course. By offering sacrifices people expected to establish a good relationship with the Overlord, to create an atmosphere of good will. The good will of the Lord would mean "rest" for his people in the deep sense of the word. Twice every day without exception the threefold offering had to be made. Leviticus 6:8, 12-13 indicates that the fire on the altar had to be perpetual. Israel was to live its life day in, day out, year after year, century after century in a spirit of surrender to God. When in later centuries the temple no longer existed and the sacrifices could no longer be offered, the spirit of surrender was expressed in songs, prayers, and deeds of faith. Thus also the Christian church is called to live a life in devotion to him who offered himself for us.

1423

OFFERINGS ON THE SABBATH 28:9-10

In the sequence of days, the Sabbath occupied a special place. Its festive character was marked by the offering of additional gifts. The regular daily offering to God's majesty was made on the Sabbath as on all days, but in addition, two male lambs and a double amount of fine flour for the homage offering, together with the appropriate drink offering, had to be brought as well. On the day of the Lord a special festive offering was indispensable.

OFFERINGS ON THE FEAST OF THE
NEW MOON 28:11-15

According to 1 Samuel 20:5, 24, and 29 the New Moon festival (the first day of the Jewish month) was a day for a common meal, which was observed either in the small circle of the family or possibly on a large scale within the clan. Also, it was a custom on that day to seek out men of God to consult them on important matters (see 2 Kings 4:23). In Amos 8:5, Hosea 2:10, and Isaiah 1:13 we find the Sabbath and the New Moon festival mentioned in the same breath. The offerings prescribed for the day were more costly than those for the Sabbath, however. The offering to God's majesty on this day required two young bulls, one ram, and seven male lambs. The homage offering required about six quarts of fine flour mixed with oil with each bull, about four quarts with the ram, and about two quarts with each of the lambs. The drink offering required about two quarts of wine with each bull, about a quart and a half with the ram, and about a quart with each of the lambs. Verse 14b concludes the instruction concerning the offerings of devotion. Verse 15 adds that a male goat was also to be sacrificed as a sin offering—a requirement present in all succeeding instructions concerning offerings on special days. And once again, all these special offerings were in addition to the daily offering to God's majesty, which had to be offered to the Lord uninterruptedly throughout the year.

PASSOVER AND THE FEAST OF UNLEAVENED
BREAD 28:16-25

Compare with this passage the corresponding instructions in Exodus 12:14-20; Leviticus 23:5-8; Deuteronomy 16:1-8; and

Ezekiel 45:21-24. The silence concerning the Passover lamb and the Passover meal is noteworthy. Verse 16 simply reports that on the fourteenth day of the first month, the month of Nisan, there was to be a Passover celebration before the Lord. Virtually all of the rest of this passage is concerned with the Feast of Unleavened Bread, which was to last seven days. It was both to begin (on the fifteenth day of the month) and end with a holy convocation. Evidently this took place in and by the sanctuary. Participants in this convocation were directed to avoid all heavy work. The offerings specified for this feast were the same as those required for the festival of the New Moon—the same offering to God's majesty, the same homage offering, and, although they are not expressly mentioned, the same drink offerings. Verse 23 says that the special offerings were to be given in addition to the normal morning offering, but verse 24 speaks of the continual offering as such and so probably includes both the morning and evening offerings. All these gifts given on the festival of Unleavened Bread are called food for the Lord, the goal of which is to secure an atmosphere of rest and peace between God and his people. And here too a sin offering proves to be necessary (v. 22). God cannot be adequately praised without the element of atonement.

THE FIRSTFRUITS AND THE FEAST OF WEEKS 28:26-31

In Leviticus 23:15-22 we read that the Feast of Weeks was to be observed precisely seven weeks—on the fiftieth day—after the offering of the sheaf of the wave offering ("fiftieth day" is rendered *pentekoste* in Greek, pointing to the connection between this feast and the New Testament Pentecost). Deuteronomy 16:9-12 also mentions seven weeks, but it specifies that the fifty days are to be counted from the first day the people put the sickle to the standing grain, and that would not have been the same everywhere. Exodus 34:22 is yet more vague, merely linking the Feast of Weeks with the firstfruits of the wheat harvest. Equally vague is Numbers 28:26, which simply refers to the day of firstfruits, the new "homage" offering, and the Feast of Weeks. The Targum Pseudo-Jonathan adds "when the seven weeks are fulfilled."

Since only one sacred convocation is prescribed, we can assume that the feast was limited to one day. In the nature of the case, heavy work would have been prohibited on this occasion. The offerings called for were precisely the same as those prescribed for the Feast of Unleavened Bread, including the male goat (the designation "as a sin offering" appears in some Hebrew manuscripts, the Samaritan text, and the Septuagint). The words "firstfruits" and "offering of new grain" are new here, indicating that this one day signaled dependence on and gratitude to him who gave the new harvest. The New Testament draws the line from the sheaf of wheat through to the greater gift of the Spirit.

THE DAY OF THE SHOUTING 29:1-6

The RSV translates verse 1c as "It is a day for you to blow the trumpets." The verb in the Hebrew can mean either "to blow" or "to shout." The same verb is used in Numbers 10:1-10, where the word for trumpet is also used, making the meaning clear. In this passage, however, the word for trumpet does not appear, and in the absence of the term, I am more inclined to translate verse 1c as "A day of shouting shall it be for you."

The word I translate as "shouting" here occurs elsewhere in the Old Testament in connection with the ark, with regard to both military activity and acts of worship. It also appears in the context of the enthronement of a new king. Applied to the service of the Lord, it connotes a jubilant acknowledgment of his eternal kingship.

The first day of the seventh month had a particularly festive character, as indicated by the larger than usual offerings prescribed for it. There were, first of all, the continual offerings to God's majesty in the morning and at twilight, along with the appropriate "homage" offerings and drink offerings. Next to be added were all the offerings to be brought on the day of the new moon. And finally, there were the offerings to be brought on the first day of the seventh month. They were the same as the offerings to God's majesty, homage offerings, and drink offerings that were brought at the preceding feast days except that only one bull was required, not two. A male goat was again required as a sin offering.

Why the abundance of prescribed offerings on this particular day of the new moon? Because the number seven made it a sabbath month? Or was this the Israelite New Year's day in the period prior to the adoption of the Babylonian calendar around 600 B.C.? We know that the day came in the fall, after the whole harvest was in. It is possible that the significance of this date as time for giving thanks might have been enriched by the addition of elements from the Babylonian tradition. The Babylonians used their New Year's day to celebrate the enthronement of their gods Marduk and Nabû and to petition them for assurances regarding the coming year. The Israelites might have shifted these emphases, celebrating the enthronement of the Lord as their supreme ruler and expressing their trust in him as the basis for sufficient assurance regarding the year to come. The abundant offerings would have been in keeping with such an emphasis. Leviticus 23:23-24 shows the same line of thought. The Targum Pseudo-Jonathan says that the shouting drove away the Satan who came to accuse Israel.

THE DAY OF ATONEMENT 29:7-11

We read next of a holy convocation to be held on the tenth day of the seventh month. This Day of Atonement is also mentioned in Leviticus 16:29-31, a passage that begins and ends with a summons to the people to deny themselves and that also contains a command to abstain from work and observe a period of rest. The point of the activities was to atone for sin and achieve a complete purification. The special day is also mentioned in Leviticus 23:26-31, which notes the requirements of self-denial, a special offering to the Lord, and the omission of all work.

Numbers 29:7-11 follows these two passages in Leviticus by speaking of a holy convocation and specifying the requirements of self-denial, a rigorous observance of rest, and a number of offerings. The Targum Pseudo-Jonathan states that the self-denial was to consist of abstention from food and drink, from the bathhouse and anointing, from wearing sandals, and from conjugal intercourse. In reality, it entailed much more; it was a call to self-discipline, a total change in attitude to deep inner repentance, penitence, and conversion that would result in one's entire life being redirected—that is, directed to God and him alone. Connected with this was the demand for an absolute observance of rest. A number of ancient translations contain somewhat less rigorous demands in this respect, simply calling for abstention from all heavy labor.

The offerings are the same as those in mentioned in verses 2-5, plus of course the continual offering to God's majesty and its accompanying features. Less clear is the meaning of "the sin offering of atonement" mentioned in verse 11b. It may have been the male goat mentioned in verse 11a, but as the RSV translation reflects, it seems more likely that it was another offering altogether. It is, after all, a prescription for the great Day of Atonement, the context that makes sense of all the other prescriptions. Atonement depends on self-denial, offerings, and rest here, just as the entire gospel rests on the atonement accomplished by the suffering and death of Jesus Christ.

THE FEAST OF TABERNACLES 29:12-40

Originally the three great feasts were probably rooted in the agricultural calendar, but in Israel they acquired another meaning. The Feast of Unleavened Bread had to do with the barley harvest, the Feast of Weeks with the ripened wheat, and the Feast of Tabernacles with the harvest of grapes and other field products. The Feast of Tabernacles had an exuberant character; in later ages it became a saying that "anyone who has not experienced the joy of the Feast of Tabernacles does not know what real joy is." One gets a sense of this exuberance from the descriptions of the feast in Leviticus 23:39-44 and Deuteronomy 16:13-15. In Leviticus 23:34-36 and Numbers 29:12-40, however, the emphasis is on the long duration of the feast—seven days plus an added day for a conclusion—as well as on the rest to be observed on the first and the eighth days, and especially on the exceptionally high number of offerings.

Numbers 29:12-40 goes on at length concerning the offerings. On the first day the offering to God's majesty was to include thirteen bulls, two rams, and fourteen male lambs. The homage offering was to consist of fine flour mixed with oil and to be given with the animals in the proportion of three parts with each bull to two parts with each ram to one part with each lamb. The drink offering was to be omitted on the first day but included on all subsequent days. On top of all this, the people were to make the two daily offerings to God's majesty along with their attendant features. On each successive day one less bull was required. The eighth day (an addition, really) was to be completely out of step: one bull, one ram, and seven male lambs. The total for the entire feast, then, was 71 bulls, 15 rams, 105 male lambs, 8 male goats, plus the appropriate homage and drink offerings, plus the normal daily offerings—a great abundance of everything!

The purpose of all this giving was to express the gratitude the people owed to God for his many gifts to them. The intent was to ensure a good relationship with him and demonstrate the people's awareness of the large place he had in their life.

Verse 39 repeats the names of the prescribed offerings once more for good measure. In addition to these, it also mentions "votive offerings" (offerings an individual had in some other context vowed to bring) and "freewill offerings" (offerings an individual had voluntarily decided to make). These voluntary offerings were to be brought in addition to those prescribed for the feast.

The prophet Zechariah envisioned the Feast of Tabernacles (eventually referred to simply as "the Feast") being destined for all the nations (Zech. 14:16-18). The book of Revelation is steeped in the atmosphere of this feast—as in chapter 7, which speaks of the great multitude that no one can number surrounding the throne and the lamb with palm branches in their hands and exuberant doxologies on their tongues.

VOWS 30:1-16

In this passage we read that Moses addressed the heads of the tribes about God's will concerning vows and pledges. Repeatedly two terms are employed—"vow" and "oath to bind oneself" (v. 2); probably the former refers to a vow to do something, and the latter refers to a pledge to abstain from doing something. Both sorts of vows could be either binding or nonbinding, depending on the circumstances under which they were made. When a man made a promise to the Lord, he was simply bound to make good on his word (v. 2). A woman, on the other hand, would be irrevocably bound to her vow or pledge only when she was not tied to either a father or a husband (v. 9 cites the widow and the divorced woman as examples). All other females, in accordance with ancient Israelite law, were subject to the authority of a man, be it father or husband, and the men had some responsibility for vows made by the women under their authority. A woman entering marriage while under obligation to a vow or a pledge constituted a special case.

The basic rule for women under a man's authority was that

the vow would remain in force if the man said nothing to the contrary—silence was reckoned as consent—but if the man objected, then responsibility for the nonfulfillment of the vow would come to rest on him and the woman would be free. God himself would absolve her. In the case of a girl who still lived at home and was subject to the authority of her father, the father would determine whether the vows were to be kept. In the case of a girl who was bound by a vow with the consent of her father while she was single but who subsequently married, her husband would assume authority for determining whether the vows were to be kept after they were married. In the case of a married woman who wanted to assume an obligation, if her husband did not oppose the commitment on the day he heard of it, it would stand. If more than twenty-four hours passed before he objected (according to the rabbinical interpretation), then the husband would become responsible. According to the Hebrew text and the RSV, he would then bear *her* iniquity; other versions (the Samaritan, the Septuagint, the Syriac) read "*his* iniquity."

The matter of vowing a vow or making a pledge was taken very seriously in Israel. If the foundation of the faith was the immovable trustworthiness of God, no wonder a premium was put on being true to one's promises in general.

VENGEANCE AGAINST MIDIAN 31:1-24

There were two reasons that the Israelites sought vengeance against the Midianites. The first was that Midian had joined with the Moabites in attempting to secure the services of Balaam to put a curse on the people of God. When that failed, the Midianites, like the Moabites, sought to ruin Israel by encouraging the men to commit idolatry. The result was the death of thousands of people. The second reason was that Midian owed a debt to God. Having induced the people of God to involve themselves in the service of Baal at Peor, the Midianites shared responsibility for Israel's unfaithfulness to the Lord. Verses 2 and 3 show that the vengeance is repayment both for their assaults against Israel and their assaults against God.

The battle—to which a thousand men per tribe were called—had the character of an execution, in the form of a *ban*. The ban was a religious institution exercised for a time in Israel as well as among some of its Semitic neighbors that placed people judged to be hostile to the deity under a sentence of destruction. We find instances of the ban in different places throughout the Old Testament, as for example in the cases of Jericho (Josh. 6-7) and the Amalekites (1 Sam. 15). The most rigorous form of the ban involved the total destruction of all of a people and all of their possessions. There were also more moderate forms that spared at least some of the people and their material possessions. But in any form, there was always something very awesome in a ban, something comparable to an execution.

A number of points in the text make it clear that the war with Midian was religious in nature. When we compare the size of the Israelite army as it is described here with the large figures elsewhere in the book of Numbers, it is conspicuously small: only twelve thousand men. A small fraction represents the whole. There is reference to commanders (v. 14) but no word about a commander-in-chief. Moses remained in the camp, and Joshua is not mentioned. Moses' accusation (v. 15) assumes that it was the officers' task to execute God's judgment on the guilty among the Midianites. Only one person is mentioned, Phinehas (v. 6), the man who in chapter 25 is said to have averted the plague from Israel by his forceful action. In the same context mention is made of the articles of the sanctuary that were necessary for religious purposes as well as of the trumpets for signaling.

The outcome of the battle was most remarkable. On the Midianite side, literally all the able-bodied men died in battle, whereas the Israelites did not lose even one man. This raises the question of whether this was in fact a military engagement or a priestly affair for executing the guilty. There is a clear line that runs from Numbers 31:1-24 to the conquest of Jericho according to Joshua 6 and 7. For in fact that city fell not by military violence but by the force of Israel's obedient faith. And the same thing is true of the conquest of Midian described in Judges 7: it was not the military might of Gideon's band that was decisive but rather the power of faith. In all three cases the stories have about them something unnatural, something unreal, something exaggerated, and in all three it was obedience to God's command that turned the tide.

Numbers 31:1-24 says little about the campaign itself. The able-bodied men on Midian's side were all destroyed. Among them were five sheiks (tribal chiefs here grandiosely called "kings"), among whom was Zur, father of Cozbi (see Num. 25:15). Also killed, remarkably enough, was Balaam. Whereas in chapters 22-24 he is presented as a man who in fact conformed himself to the will of the Lord and blessed the people of Israel, the Targum Pseudo-Jonathan, speaking of the advice he gave Balak in Numbers 24:14, states that he was a dangerous deceiver, formulating a plan to undermine the faith of the Israelites: "Go, make ready the inns, install prostitutes who sell food and drink below cost. And they, this people, will come and eat and drink, and become drunk, and sleep with them, and deny their God." As Numbers 25 demonstrates, this scheme was unfortunately successful. Revelation 2:14 also refers to this event: "Balaam . . . taught Balak to put a stumbling block before the sons of Israel, that they might eat food sacrificed to idols and practice immorality." This is the view of Balaam that underlies Numbers 31:8. He is evil incarnate. Hence the fanciful history concerning him in the Targum Pseudo-Jonathan. He is reported to have used magical tricks to attempt to escape from the death penalty, but Phinehas proved superior to him and killed him with the sword.

After the battle, the Israelite army returned with an enormous amount of plunder in people, animals, and material possessions. Elsewhere in the Old Testament we read that the women and girls went out to meet the conquerors with festive songs (see, e.g., Judg. 11:34; 1 Sam. 18:6); verse 13 of this passage says that in this case it was Moses, Eleazar, and the leaders of the people who went out to meet the warriors. Sadly, the meeting turned into a bitter disappointment. Moses became angry because those who were especially guilty—the women and the daughters of the Moabites and apparently also of the Midianites who persuaded the Israelite men to serve Baal-Peor—had been spared. He demanded that the death penalty be imposed on all females who had had sexual intercourse with a man.

In verses 19 and following, rules for passing from a state of war to that of ordinary life are presented. The men who had been in contact with dead bodies were instructed to remain outside the camp for a week. On the third and seventh days they would have to purify themselves. Also the material goods, to which the impurity of death and corruption clung, had to be cleansed. In verses 21-24 we read that Eleazar passed on a number of rules that had to be followed in the process. Metals had to be cleansed by fire; everything that would burn had to be cleansed with water. A parenthetical statement in verse 23 refers to the water of cleansing mentioned in Numbers 19. After having been completely cleansed of every stain, the warriors could return to the camp after a week. The God of Israel is the God of life.

THE SPOILS ARE DIVIDED 31:25-54

Verses 25-54 combine two distinct matters—the spoils due the people and the spoils due God. The spoils due the people had to be equitably divided, and to this end a rule resembling that followed by David (see 1 Sam. 30:24) was applied. The spoils as a whole were divided in two equal parts. One half went to those who actually took part in the fighting, and the other half went to the overwhelming majority who stayed in the camp. As for the share due the Lord, the warriors were instructed to surrender one five hundredth of the spoils, which is the share which the Lord gave to the priests. The majority of the people were instructed to surrender one fiftieth of their share. The Lord gave this part to the Levites. So the proportion of the priests' share to that of the Levites was one to ten, approximately the same as the proportion specified in chapter 18.

On the basis of the figures given in this chapter we therefore get the following result:

	total	one-half	the priests' share	the Levites' share
sheep	675,000	337,500	675	6,750
cattle	72,000	36,000	72	720
donkeys	61,000	30,500	61	610
people	32,000	16,000	32	320

See verses 32-40. The text does not record the figures for the Levites' share, but it is of course fixed.

Verses 48-54 report on the offering of the commanders of the various divisions, which consisted of a variety of gold ornaments that the wives of nomads typically wore.

The Targum Pseudo-Jonathan offers the information that

the Israelites were not persuaded by the beauty of the Midianite girls and women but only took their diadems, earrings, neck chains, armbands, finger rings, and pendants. According to verse 54, the total weight amounted to 16,750 shekels of gold. The precise weight of the shekel is uncertain; it varied over time and from place to place. The shekel mentioned here, though, is estimated to have weighed approximately two-fifths of an ounce, making the total weight of the offering something more than 418 pounds—clearly a huge amount. According to verse 53, the rank and file of the soldiers kept the plunder for themselves, evidently having received permission to do so.

Verse 50 reports that this costly offering of gold was given "to make atonement . . . before the Lord." Are we to understand that the commanders had to atone for their initial failure to carry out the sentence? Or was an atonement necessary after every military engagement because people had been killed? Or was it a necessary step in the return to ordinary life? Whatever the case, this costly offering obviously served to remove some guilt that weighed on the warriors.

This element of atonement is underscored by the reference to the place where the commanders brought their gift through the mediation of Moses and Eleazar—namely, the tent of meeting. There it was given as a memorial before the face of the Lord in Israel's favor, in order that he might remain gracious to his people. At the same time the gift reminded the people to direct their thoughts to him. It was thus a memorial proceeding from God and proceeding from Israel.

GAD, REUBEN, AND THE HALF TRIBE OF MANASSEH 32:1-42

In verse 1 the sons of Reuben are mentioned before the sons of Gad, but in subsequent references this order is reversed. The reason is very likely that the tribe of Gad was more important than that of Reuben. There is an oblique confirmation of this supposition on a stone that King Mesha of Moab set up around 850 B.C., following his defeat of the Israelites. This stone bears an inscription that refers to Gad as a people that lived there from times immemorial. A number of other names listed in verses 3 and 34-42 also found their way onto the stone.

According to verses 1-5, the two tribes that owned large herds of cattle noticed how well-suited the newly conquered territories east of the Jordan were for grazing cattle. There is an Arab proverb that names the area as ideal for raising cattle. For this reason they asked Moses, Eleazar, and the other leaders that the "land of Gilead" be allotted to them. They viewed this area as their ultimate goal and felt no need to travel further westward beyond the Jordan. Their request implies that they felt no need to fight alongside the other tribes for possession of the promised land. If they could have this land, the other tribes could proceed on their own.

Moses' reaction (vv. 6-15) was particularly intense. Behind this request of the two tribes he sensed the same mentality as that of the spies in chapters 13 and 14. They also judged the fulfillment of God's promise to be impossible. They proposed instead to return to the fruitful river delta of Egypt. Now the tribes of Gad and Reuben were in effect saying that God's promise concerning Canaan was unimportant, that they would be satisfied with the land of Gilead. If they were given their way, who would guarantee that soon all the other tribes, which also possessed cattle, would not make the same kind of demands? If in this way the people were going to trample on God's promises afresh, the former history would repeat itself. This generation, too, would experience the wrath of God exploding over it, would perish in the wilderness and pasture lands east of the Jordan, the door to the promised land slammed shut in their faces. In verses 14-15 we read that Moses flatly accused the Gadites and Reubenites of being a brood of sinful men who would be the ruin of all the people.

Verses 16-19 report that the two tribes responded to these sharp words of Moses by promising to cross the Jordan along with the others, armed to do battle—or, as the Hebrew has it, "as swift warriors." More than that, they would enter ahead of the others. And they would go back only when all the other tribes had reached their destination and God's promise had been fulfilled. In this promise a very different mentality comes through. No longer were they implying that they would be satisfied if only they got their share; rather, the message that comes through is, "We are together *one* people; we live by only *one* promise and are led by *one* God." A total inner turn-about had taken place. Of course, they would first have to secure the safety of the women, the children, and the cattle. For that purpose they would need fortified cities and corrals made of loose stones piled on top of each other, like a wall around the flocks.

Verses 20-27 report that Moses accepted their promise, and the two tribes repeated their commitment. Striking, in Moses' words, is the repeated phrase "before the Lord." All that was going to happen—the passage through the Jordan, the defeat of their adversaries, the conquest of the land—all would take place before the Lord. If Gad and Reuben kept their word, they could look forward to dwelling in the territory of Gilead with a good conscience. But if they broke their promise, they would be guilty before the Lord and would experience the consequences of their breach of faith in their lives: their sin would find them out.

Verses 28-32 roughly repeat the preceding. When Canaan was conquered, Moses would no longer be present. For that reason Eleazar, Joshua, and the leaders of the tribes would have to see to it that the promise was kept. The punishment for the two tribes should they fail to keep their promise was that they would have to live among the other tribes, and there would be no telling how large their territory would be in such a case.

Verses 34-38 list the names of the cities that were to be built or rebuilt by the Gadites and the Reubenites. The location of some of them is known to us. From the available data we can deduce that the tribe of Reuben occupied a relatively small area around the ancient city of Heshbon. Around that lay the land of the Gadites, extending in all directions, with the Arnon as the southern boundary, the Dead Sea and the Jordan as the western boundary, the Jabbok as the northern boundary, and the land of the Ammonites as the eastern boundary. In the course of the following centuries, these boundaries were altered from time to time.

The references to the half tribe of Manasseh in verses 33-42 are somewhat problematic. The Samaritan text mentions Gad, Reuben, and Manasseh throughout the entire chapter, but the Hebrew text does this only in verse 33. The passage appears to constitute a very distinct tradition, one that is sometimes hard to harmonize with verses 1-32. The style of verses 33-42 is quite different as well. The passage indicates that Machir, the son of Manasseh, drove out the Amorites from Gilead and took up residence there; that Jair, another son of Manasseh, captured a number of tent settlements and named them after himself (Havvoth-jair, RSV); and that Nobah, possibly also a son of Manasseh, took possession of Kenath and surrounding settlements and called them Nobah. Reference is made in verse 39 to the sons of Machir, and in verse 40 to Machir himself, but the two are equivalent: to the eastern mind the patriarch and his descendants are identical. In any case, there was also a tradition concerning a part of Manasseh that settled in the land of Gilead. Could it be that in later years they migrated from the west to the east?

THE JOURNEY THROUGH THE WILDERNESS 33:1-49

In this passage we find a list of the stopping places on Israel's journey, beginning from the time of the exodus on the fifteenth day of the first month after the Passover. While the Egyptians were busy burying their first-born, the Israelites started their journey under the protection of the Lord. Verse 4b shows a glimpse of the background. There was more involved in this incident than a mere conflict between the mighty nation on the Nile and the slave people in the delta. At bottom it was a decisive conflict between the gods of the highly developed culture of Egypt and the God of Israel. The Targum Pseudo-Jonathan correctly notes that the idols of cast metal melted, the idols of stone were shattered, the idols of clay were broken in pieces, the idols of wood were reduced to ashes, and the animal deities died. In this perspective the events are on the highest possible level.

This list contains a summary of things we find elsewhere in Exodus and Numbers, but it also contains some items that are referred to only here. According to verse 2, this material was put down in writing by Moses at the Lord's command. Some very ancient documents composed in a similar style have been preserved. The style, characteristic of such documents, features the continually repeated formula "they set out from place X and encamped at place Y." We know of similar lists constructed by nomadic Arabs living today, but they existed in antiquity as well, as the inscriptions of the Assyrian kings testify.

Especially important are the beginning (Egypt) and the end (the fords of the Jordan across from Jericho). Also of key importance is Mount Sinai, which many scholars locate at the south point of the Sinai peninsula but which may have been located much farther to the north, in the neighborhood of Kadesh-barnea. Some scholars place it to the northeast of the Gulf of Aqabah. And finally, there is Kadesh-barnea, a place situated at a point where the wildernesses of Sur, Paran, and Sin meet at Mount Seir, a central oasis from which the people made further journeys and on which they could fall back whenever necessary. Regrettably, we cannot identify most of the places on the list today, and so it is impossible to determine the exact route that Israel followed. Only the first and the last part have been identified with some certainty, telling us that the people traveled from south to north through the land of Moab.

This sober recital is interrupted in places by clarifications, additions, and expansions. Verse 8 tells us that a journey of three days followed the passage through the Red Sea. Is this a reminder of Exodus 8:20, where Moses asks permission from Pharaoh to go and celebrate a feast before the Lord in the wilderness? Verse 9 says that there were twelve springs and seventy palm trees in Elim. (The Targum Pseudo-Jonathan takes this to signify that Elim contained twelve tribes and seventy wise men—a questionable interpretation.) Verse 14 contains a note pertaining to a lack of water. Verses 38-39 refer to events recorded in 20:23-29, where the record speaks of the death of Aaron on the first day of the fifth month in the fortieth year. Verse 40 is reminiscent of 21:1-3. Verse 49 shows the people standing on the threshold of the promised land: God's promise is being fulfilled. For the rest, we must not, as does the Targum Pseudo-Jonathan, look for deeper meanings in these names.

ISRAEL AND CANAAN 33:50-56

This passage reads as though it could have been taken right from Deuteronomy 7:2-6. It breathes the same spirit, it warns against the same danger, and it is charged with the same concern. The point is that the land of Canaan is a gift from God to Israel. The people could possess it, dwell in it, and live in peace. In dividing it the people had to act in accordance with the fairness rule as well as by the outcome of the lot (v. 54; cf. 26:52-56). But the people would endure only if God occupied first place in their lives. He wanted to be their God, but they had to realize that they were totally his.

The fact that the Israelites were God's people so determined the whole of their existence that any form of idolatry was by definition excluded. There was no room for paganism, half-paganism, or irresponsible tolerance. All links with paganism had to be severed. Everything on which it rested and fed had to be swept aside. A radical reformation was required. In practice this meant that the idols of the pagans had to be destroyed, the metal images pulverized, the shrines (the so-called "high places") demolished (v. 52). Only the service of the living God was permitted.

If Israel were to refuse to take such radical steps, if it were to allow paganism to go on undisturbed, then the Lord promised to reverse the order. The things he had brought on the Canaanites would be brought on his own people. They would suffer in Canaan at the hands of its pagan inhabitants the sorts of torments they had suffered at the hands of the Egyptians. The Canaanites would be as "barbs in their eyes" and "thorns in their sides." Anyone who takes the trouble to read Israel's history from shortly after the entry up to the second fall of Jerusalem in A.D. 70 will discover how seriously the Lord meant these words.

THE BOUNDARIES OF THE PROMISED LAND 34:1-12

Since we do not know the present locations of most of the places referred to in this passage, we must be satisfied, as we consider the boundaries of the promised land, with a general impression.

The southern border ran in a southwesterly direction from the Salt Sea (= the Dead Sea) in the east to Akrabbim (the Scorpion Pass), through the wilderness of Zin, issuing in the important oasis area of Kadesh-barnea by way of Hazar-addar and Azmon (whose location we cannot establish with certainty), on to the Brook of Egypt (Wadi el-Arish), ending at last at the Mediterranean. This line runs somewhat to the south of the border of the tribes of Judah and Simeon.

The western boundary is formed by the Great Sea (the Mediterranean). It must be noted here that it was not until the time of the Maccabees—after 165 B.C.—that the Israelites actually gained possession of the coastal area (1 Macc. 14:5). Before that time the Philistines controlled the entire southern strip, and the Phoenicians controlled the northern part. Not much of it was left for Israel.

The northern boundary ran from the Mediterranean Sea to Mount Hor (not to be confused with the mountain in the southern desert where Aaron died). From there "to the entrance of Hamath" (literally, Lebo-Hamath), it passed through Zedad, Ziphron, and Hazar-enan. There is some uncertainty about the meaning of Lebo-Hamath. If it means "the way to Hamath," then the reference would be to the beginning of a road that ended at Hamath, which would suggest that the northern boundary was close to the one between present-day Israel and Lebanon. Zedad, Ziphron, and Hazar-enan would have been somewhere to the east. On the other hand, if Lebo-Hamath does not mean "the way to Hamath" but simply specified a place name, then the northern boundary would have been much farther to the north, perhaps around the present boundary between Lebanon and Syria. If that were the case, then Zedad, Ziphron, and Hazar-enan would of course also have been further north.

The description of the eastern boundary ties in with that of the northern boundary, starting with Hazar-enan, running to Shepham, down to Riblah (not to be confused with the large city on the Orontes River to the north), skirting the shores of the sea of Chinnereth (= the Sea of Galilee), going down to the Jordan, and then running straight south to the Dead Sea. With this last lap the circle is complete.

The precise significance of this description of the boundaries remains in question, however. The list of names in these verses (assuming the northern boundary to coincide with the present border between Israel and Lebanon) corresponds rather well with historical reality and agrees with the much-used expression "from Dan to Beer-sheba": Dan was situated close to Mount Hermon, and Beer-sheba lay within the borders of Judah. But there are other texts in the Old Testament that speak of a much larger area. For instance, Genesis 15:18 describes the promised land as stretching "from the river of Egypt to the great river"—that is, from the Nile to the Euphrates. Such passages as Deuteronomy 11:24 and Joshua 1:4 roughly agree with this: "Your territory shall be from the wilderness to Lebanon and from the River, the river Euphrates, to the western sea." Accepting the more northern location of Lebo-Hamath would put us closer to describing this larger area.

The later Jewish idea, as it comes to expression in the Targum Pseudo-Jonathan, goes much further. It suggests that the southern boundary ran from the Dead Sea to the Nile; that the western boundary embraced the primeval ocean (of which the Mediterranean is a part) along with all the territories that belong to it, including islands, cities, harbors, and ships; that the northern boundary extended from the Cilician Gate in Asia Minor to Damascus; and that the eastern boundary included, at the very least, the entire Trans-Jordan up to the Dead Sea.

A text from Qumran goes still further. In it we read how the patriarch Abraham started out at the Nile, walked along the Mediterranean to the Amanus, reached the Euphrates River, went down to the Persian Gulf, traversed the entire Arabian peninsula, and went back to Egypt along the Red Sea, thereby surveying much of the known world, all of which was the promised land.

The early Christian interpreters understood the promise to include not only the entire earth but also heaven. The kingdom of God embraces everything, but that is a fulfillment that goes far beyond the promise, a fulfillment as large as that kingdom in which God will be all in all (1 Cor. 15:28).

THE DIVISION OF THE LAND 34:13-29

Since Moses himself would not enter the promised land, the division of Canaan west of the Jordan had to be entrusted to Eleazar, who was to cast the lots, and Joshua, the future commander-in-chief. They were assisted by ten representatives of the tribes. Apart from Caleb, none of these persons has been mentioned before. This is, of course, in keeping with the fact that the whole preceding generation died in the wilderness. None of their names incorporates the divine name YHWH, though the name El (God) appears in several. According to verses 13-15 the tribes Gad, Reuben, and the half tribe Manasseh had already received their inheritance east of the Jordan. This report corresponds with chapter 32. Canaan proper therefore fell to nine and a half tribes. It is striking, therefore, that verse 23 still refers to Manasseh as a single whole. Obviously, there are two traditions next to each other here—one more reason for thinking that a part of Manasseh later went east.

The names of the ten tribes occur in a south-north order, with Dan being listed between Benjamin and Manasseh. This is in keeping with what we read in Judges 13-16: the Danite Samson lived close to the territory of the Philistines. Only later did this tribe move north (Judges 18). The tribe of Levi is not mentioned, but of course the Levites constituted a special case.

THE CITIES OF THE LEVITES 35:1-8

The priests of the Egyptians, the Mesopotamians, and the Hittites had huge possessions in land, but this was not the case in ancient Israel. The tribe of Levi, to which both priests and Levites belonged, did not share in the distribution of the land. They were dependent for their livelihood on the revenues of the sacrifices and the yield of their possessions in cattle, although the other tribes were obliged to help them, in accordance with the rule recorded in verse 8: the strongest shoulders must bear the heaviest burdens. Verse 7 says that the Levites were to be given forty-eight cities together with the pasture land around them, but it is not clear from verses 1-8 whether they were technically to be counted as the possession of the cult servants. In Leviticus 25:32-34, however, we read that both houses and pasture lands remained the possession of the Levites.

Scholars disagree on what size these pasture lands may have been. The Hebrew text is not entirely clear on this point. Verse 4 speaks of pasture land extending one thousand cubits (1,500 feet) from the walls of the city, and verse 5 speaks of land extending two thousand cubits (3,000 feet) from the city walls. The Septuagint harmonizes the verse by converting the figure in verse 4 to two thousand cubits. I believe we can best understand the text to be indicating that the first 1,500 feet of land surrounding the city walls was to belong to the Levites and that the next 1,500 feet of land beyond that was to be open to the use of all the other Israelites. This would have made the best possible provision for the servants of the sanctuary.

In Joshua 21 we find extensive reference to the towns and the pasture lands set aside for the Levites. This ensured that the Israelites had people who would offer their lives in the service of the Lord and who would lead them and build them up in the faith living among them throughout the land. Such functions were the raison d'être of the tribe of Levi.

THE CITIES OF REFUGE 35:9-34

Verses 9-15 set out the general rules pertaining to the cities of refuge that were to be established after the entry. There were to be six in all, three on either side of the Jordan. The intent was to reach a balance between the justice that demands the death penalty for the murderer and the mercy that demands leniency in the case of unintentional homicide.

By the standards of Israel's law, human life was so precious that a murderer absolutely had to be punished. The person under obligation to execute the death sentence was the victim's next-of-kin, the so-called "avenger" or "blood-redeemer." He was entitled to kill the murderer wherever and whenever he found him, provided it was outside a city of refuge. A man who had killed another by accident, however, could escape this avenger by fleeing to a city of refuge, where he would be granted asylum until the popular assembly had determined in a court session whether he had acted maliciously or innocently. This rule applied across the board to Israelites, to strangers who had limited rights, and to sojourners, who had rights roughly comparable to those of aliens staying in modern Western countries on work visas.

Verses 16-29 work out the general rule, beginning with examples of different kinds of homicide. One could kill someone with an iron object (this presupposes the transition from the Bronze to the Iron Age), with a stone, or with a wooden object. It could be done by stabbing the victim or throwing an object at him or hitting him. The motives mentioned include hatred, malice, and hostility. The motive was decisive for settling the question of whether the killer had acted intentionally. It was possible, after all, that a killer would have fostered no hatred whatsoever, had no evil intentions whatever, or even have been a friend of the victim. The community had to decide. I believe that the community being referred to here was the community from which both the killer and his victim came. In the first place, this community would have been best able to judge how the two persons had related to each other in the past. In the small communities of ancient Israel everyone knew everyone else. In the second place, verse 25 mentions that the accused could be sent back to the city of refuge after he had been summoned from that city to stand trial in an orderly way; presumably the trial would have taken place among his own people.

When the investigation indicated that the murder had been premeditated, the judge would pronounce the verdict with a fixed formula: "He is a murderer." The death sentence, which irrevocably followed, was also pronounced with a fixed formula: "He shall be put to death." That verdict would remove the murderer from the protection of the law and make him liable to execution at the hands of the avenger at any time and any place. The city of refuge would no longer offer him any protection. If on the other hand there was nothing in his past or in the circumstances in which the homicide occurred to suggest that there had been bad blood between the killer and his victim, then the community would be justified in returning the accused to the city of refuge, where he would be totally safe from the avenger. He would be judged innocent of real murder and therefore not have to suffer punishment. The only condition placed on his freedom was that he would have to remain in the city of refuge as long as the high priest in office was alive. If he were to leave the city before that time he would run the risk of still being killed by the avenger—and the avenger would be considered justified in having executed him.

The three passages in the Old Testament that discuss the cities of refuge at length (Deut. 19:1-13; Josh. 20:1-9; and Num. 35:9-34) each have their own emphasis. Numbers 35:25-28 mentions the death of the high priest. This may have been because not all cities of refuge were cities of the Levites (although the reverse is not true). The high priest was the highest person in rank in the tribe of Levi. When he died, the bond with the Levitical tribe would in a sense be broken, and the bond with the city of refuge would be broken as well. It is also possible that the passing of the high priest was taken to mark the conclusion of one period in the history of Israel and the incorporation of a new high priest was taken to begin a new period. Or it may have been that the death of the high priest was presumed to have an expiatory effect even for those who were subjectively not guilty. Whatever the case, the ruling was that after the death of the high priest, the man who had unintentionally killed someone could return to his original home without any threat to his life.

Verses 30-32 offer a few additions. First, a capital case was not left to the decision of one person. The entire community had to be involved, with official agencies deciding. Further, the testimony of one person was not sufficient for a conviction. There had to be at least two witnesses (cf. Deut. 19:15). Furthermore, it was strictly forbidden to buy off a blood debt with money. The value of a human life prohibited it. On this point the Israelite law is strikingly different from Mesopotamian law, which permitted this sort of bargain. Finally, it was absolutely forbidden to accept a payment from someone who wanted to leave the city of refuge before his time was up. In Israel only strict and pure justice was valid.

Verses 33 and 34 touch upon the heart of the issue. It was a great and gracious gift of the Lord that he should have lived among his people. So far as Israel was concerned—and so far as we are concerned—his presence changed the land fundamentally, transformed it from something neutral to the dwelling place of God. This is one more reason God calls on his people not to defile the the earth with blood guilt. Such guilt can be expiated only by the blood of the guilty.

But we ought also to take account here of the fact that a gracious God can forgive a murderer like David (2 Sam. 12:13) and open paradise to an unknown criminal on a cross (Luke 23:43). His grace in Jesus Christ transcends even the requirements of justice. But *that* is a miracle.

THE MARRIAGE OF FEMALE HEIRS 36:1-13

In Numbers 27:1-6 we read of the ruling that in the absence of male heirs, daughters could inherit property. But this passage reports that the heads of families belonging to the clan of Gilead (which belongs to the tribe of Manasseh) pointed out a danger lurking in this ruling. If female heirs were to marry men of another tribe, then their inheritance would pass to the tribe of which these men were members. In the case these men cited, this would lead to a loss of land for the tribe of Manasseh. And since, according to Leviticus 25, the laws concerning the Year of Jubilee required that any land that had fallen into other hands had to return to the original owners, this set of circumstances could lead to a permanent loss. Though the women were the rightful owners, they had become members by marriage of another tribe. The men lodged their complaint before Moses and the other leaders.

Verses 5-6 make it clear that their complaint was well-founded. At the Lord's behest, Moses ruled in the matter. The daughters of Zelophehad were to receive their inheritance on condition that they would marry men belonging to their own tribe. Only in this way would the inheritance remain the possession of the descendants of Manasseh. This arrangement safeguarded the interests both of the female heirs and the other members of their tribe. The Lord had given all the land to all the people. Every tribe had received a share. Within the tribes the clans had a share allotted to them, as did, ultimately, the families. Since all had to live off the land, this sort of land allocation was necessary to ensure that each tribe had what it needed to live. And it had to remain this way.

According to verses 10-12, the five daughters of Zelophehad accepted offers of marriage from their cousins and thus kept the inheritance within the tribe, where it belonged.

In verses 8-9 we read that the ruling for the daughters of Zelophehad became a general rule. Female heirs were obligated from this time on to marry the men of their own tribe. The ties between a tribe and its land had to remain firm.

The entire book of Numbers concludes with verse 13, which underscores the fact that behind all the commands and regulations of the law was the Lord himself. By the mediation of Moses this law came to the Israelites. The foundation of all these commands lay in the time before the entry.

524